The Collegiate Athlete At Risk

Strategies for Academic Support and Success

The Collegiate Athlete At Risk

Strategies for Academic Support and Success

edited by

Morris R. Council III
University of West Georgia

Samuel R. Hodge
The Ohio State University

Robert A. Bennett III
Denison University

INFORMATION AGE PUBLISHING, INC.
Charlotte, NC • www.infoagepub.com

Library of Congress Cataloging-in-Publication Data

CIP record for this book is available from the Library of Congress
http://www.loc.gov

ISBNs: 978-1-64113-414-9 (Paperback)

978-1-64113-415-6 (Hardcover)

978-1-64113-416-3 (ebook)

Printed in the United States of America

CONTENTS

INTRODUCTION AND OVERVIEW

Samuel R. Hodge
The Ohio State University

Robert A. Bennett III
Denison University

Morris R. Council III
University of West Georgia

Major intercollegiate athletics has become synonymous with big business as a result of the billions of dollars of revenue generated by the athletic achievements of student-athletes (Carson & Rinehart, 2010; Sinclair & Bennett, 2015). This commitment to high-stakes entertainment has often come with the common understanding some student-athletes who contribute to the success of their institutions will ultimately leave them as casualties of the business. In other words, many student-athletes who present significant academic and/or social risk factors prior to entering into their institutions find their athletic contributions to the institution to be significantly more valuable than the quality of their respected educational outcomes.

The Collegiate Athlete At Risk:
Strategies for Academic Support and Success, pp. vii–xii
Copyright © 2019 by Information Age Publishing
All rights of reproduction in any form reserved.

Many scholars and practitioners have critically assessed why certain students fail to achieve academically. There findings explore many factors including race and ethnicity (Beamon, 2008; Bennett, Hodge, Graham, & Moore, 2015); identity (Bimper, 2014; Murphy, Petitpas, & Brewer, 1996; Hodge, Burden, Robinson, & Bennett, 2008; Lally & Kerr, 2005); motivation (Gaston-Gayles, 2004); demands of intercollegiate athletics (Aries, 2004; Maloney & McCormick, 1993); and academic readiness (Clark & Parette, 2002; Council, Robinson, Bennett, & Moody, 2015; Preece et al., 2007). There has been a wealth of scholarship that explores the experiences of collegians in the realm of athletics. However, there still remains a significant gap in the research to practice continuum in regards to strategies used to support student-athletes who are academically at risk.

The athletic and academic demands of student-athletes are well documented and the vast majority of National Collegiate Athletic Association (NCAA) affiliated institutions have some level of academic or holistic student-athlete support services available to mitigate the risk to underprepared student-athletes (Gaston-Gayles, 2003; Gerdy 1997). Services provided for these students typically include, academic advising, tutoring, mentoring, and counseling (Clark & Parette, 2002; Council et al., 2015; Gaston-Gayles, 2003), but the reality is many student-athletes who begin their careers most at-risk academically often fail to effectively benefit from the services and programs in place to support them. Access without effective support is not opportunity. Unfortunately, far too many student-athletes enter their respective institutions of higher education "at risk." As a result, a disproportionate number of them fail to graduate and matriculate to postbaccalaureate careers in lieu of the fact they maximized (and sometimes strained) the supports available to them.

This book is a resource that meets the educational needs of collegiate student-athletes by providing effective academic and social strategies to the individuals who support them. It utilizes evidence-based instructional strategies proven to support the success of adolescents who are at-risk in secondary settings (e.g., high school) and help adapt them to resources for college athletes at-risk of academic failure. The majority of academic advisors reported they advise students-athletes with disabilities with limited or no training on how to best support these learners (Preece et al., 2007). In fact, the overwhelming number of personnel tasked to support student-athletes who demonstrate academic risk hold no credential to support their qualification to effectively execute their positions. The attributes of adolescents who demonstrate academic risk and/or have been diagnosed with disabilities are consistent across secondary to postsecondary settings and are only amplified by the added effects of collegiate athletics. Research shows students with disabilities are more likely to enter college underprepared, take remedial courses, and are less likely to self-advocate (Madaus,

Banerjee, & Merchant, 2011) nor be proactive in making career decisions (Rojewski & Gregg, 2011). Unfortunately, many practitioners who work directly with student-athletes are quick to label them as lazy, unmotivated, and uncommitted without having a deeper understanding of them as individuals. For example, scholarship illustrates successful adolescent readers, depending on the difficulty of the text, typically read orally between 120 to 170 correct words per minute (Tindal, Hasbrouk, & Jones, 2005). If a student-athletes enters their institution reading well below grade level (e.g., 50 correct words per minute), it would be extremely difficult for them to get through 12 credit hours of college-level reading assignments regardless of their effort. This book provides clarity to why student-athletes struggle academically and effective strategies to support their success.

OVERVIEW OF CHAPTERS

The book is comprised of seven informative chapters that address the multifaceted aspects of the realities student-athletes at risk face. In Chapter 1, "Identifying and Transitioning Student-Athletes with Risk Labels and High Incidence Disabilities," Susie C. Bruhin and Lori S. Robinson conceptualize and define the term *at-risk* as it pertains to student-athletes' academic success. Further, they discuss commonly shared characteristics of at-risk student-athletes. The main purpose of this chapter is to establish a practical guide for identifying and transitioning those deemed at-risk into the collegiate environment. The authors provide a rationale for the importance of identification, communication, timing, and advocacy in supporting student-athletes who are at-risk as they transition into the collegiate setting. Lastly, Bruhin and Robinson state identification, evaluation, communication, and advocacy contribute to the success of the charge of these institutions and create a team-focused approach to student-athlete support.

In Chapter 2, "Current Models of Student-Athlete Academic Support Services" by Robert A. Bennett III and Stephon H. Fuqua discuss the history and growth of academic support for student-athletes across divisions and conferences. They also examine the various models designed for academic support and resources available to student-athletes.

The authors of the third chapter, "Developing Effective Self-Advocacy Skills in Student-Athletes With Disabilities," Morris R. Council III and Ralph Gardner III, present self-advocacy strategies as effective methods for academic support staffs to improve educational outcomes for student-athletes with disabilities. The authors provide a rationale for why these students can benefit from self-advocacy training and explore approaches to improve student-athlete utilization of disability support services.

"Measuring Academic Success: How the Standardization of Evaluating Academic Achievement Leaves Students At-Risk Behind" serves as the fourth chapter. Emily M. Newell and Morris R. Council III provide an overview of how schools measure academic success, with a focus on the NCAA and other intercollegiate governing bodies such as the National Association of Intercollegiate Athletics (NAIA) and the National Junior College Athletic Association (NJCAA). They also discuss the frustration between contingencies required to promote eligibility and the belief those contingencies alone fail to promote a positive educational experience. Finally, Newell and Council examine if traditional assessments are meaningful enough to capture the progress of student athletes who are at risk academically. Recommendations for improved evaluation of student success and success of support offices are provided.

Chapter 5, "Motivating Student-Athletes for Academic Success," Joy Gaston Gayles, Robert Lang, and Ezinne Ofoegubu asserts sustaining one's motivation for success in both academics and athletics can be a daunting reality, particularly for those student-athletes who do not have adequate institutional support and guidance. In this chapter, Gaston Gayles and colleagues focus on strategies to improve student-athletes' motivation towards academic success by first discussing some of the challenges they face related to academic standards and degree attainment. Next, they focus on the growing body of literature on motivation and student-athletes. The chapter's authors conclude with a discussion of potential strategies to motivate student-athletes for academic success.

In Chapter 6, "Response to Intervention (RtI) as a Framework for Innovation," Morris R. Council III and Mary R. Sawyer explain response to intervention (RtI) is a popular approach designed for K–12 school settings to systematically ensure learners who present with learning and behavioral needs receive individualized, scientifically validated instruction prior to being referred to special education. Further, the authors explain the framework is recognized as a tiered, preventative academic model that structures the provision of increasingly intensive interventions to students at-risk for academic failure before they fail. Council and Sawyer propose RtI as an innovative, efficient structure to revolutionize the provision of collegiate academic support for student-athletes. Although most offices of student-athlete support services utilize systems that screen and provide support (e.g., learning specialists, academic counselors) beyond what is available to non-athletic students, far too many student-athletes who present risk factors early in their collegiate careers fail to reach graduation or transition away from intensive support on the path to graduation. Offices of student athlete support should use an RtI framework to strategically match the individual's level of need to the intensity of services provided, exclaim

Council III and Sawyer. The authors assert doing so will facilitate greater academic success among student-athletes.

Chapter 7, "Staying Engaged: Faculty Mentoring Student-Athletes," Darren D. Kelly and Robert A. Bennett III explore the potential for faculty and staff members to serve as mentors to collegiate student-athletes. Kelly and Bennett III give particular attention to mentoring high profile, at-risk Black male student-athletes at large, predominantly White colleges and universities. They discuss the role mentoring can play in the lives of student-athletes, and how programming can be designed to enhance the college experience, all of which logically leads to increased graduation rates and postgraduate outcomes, while increasing retention rates and assisting with student-athlete development (i.e., psychosocial well-being, identity development, and relationship building).

REFERENCES

Aries, E. A. (2004). Comparison of athletes and nonathletes at highly selective colleges: Academic performance and personal development. *Research in Higher Education, 45*(6), 577–602.

Beamon, K. K. (2008). Used goods: Former African American college student-athletes' perception of exploitation by Division I universities. *Journal of Negro Education, 77*(4), 352–364.

Bennett, R. A., III, Hodge, S. R., Graham, D. L., & Moore III, J. L. (Eds.). (2015). *Black males and intercollegiate athletics: An exploration of problems and solutions.* Bingley, England: Emerald Group Publishing Limited.

Bimper, A. Y., Jr. (2014). Game changers: The role athletic identity and racial identity play on academic performance. *Journal of College Student Development, 55*(8), 795–807.

Carson, L. C. I. I., & Rinehart, M. A. (2010, January 1). The big business of college game day. *Texas Review of Entertainment and Sports Law, 12*(1), 1–12.

Clark, M., & Parette, P. (2002). Student athletes with learning disabilities: A model for effective supports. *College Student Journal, 36*(1), 47–62.

Council M. R., III, Robinson, L. S., Bennett R. A., III, & Moody, P. M. (2015). Black male academic support staff: Navigating the issues with Black student athletes. In R. A. Bennett III, S. R. Hodge., D. L. Graham, & J. L. Moore III (Eds.), *Black males and intercollegiate athletics: An exploration of problems and solutions* (pp. 69–89). London, England: Emerald Publishing.

Gaston-Gayles, J. L. (2003). Advising student athletes: An examination of academic support programs with high graduation rates. *NACADA Journal, 23*(1&2), 50–57.

Gaston-Gayles, J. L. (2004). Examining academic and athletic motivation among student athletes at a Division I university. *Journal of College Student Development, 45*(1), 75–83.

Gerdy, J. R. (1997). *The successful college athletic program: The new standard.* Phoenix, AZ: American Council on Education/Oryx Press.

Hodge, S. R., Burden, Jr., J. W., Robinson, L. E., & Bennett, R. A., III. (2008). Commentary on the stereotyping of Black male student-athletes: Issues and implications. *Journal for the Study of Sports and Athletes in Education*, 2(2), 203–226.

Lally, P. S., & Kerr, G. A. (2005). The career planning, athletic identity, and student role identity of intercollegiate student athletes. *Research Quarterly for Exercise and Sport*, 76(3), 275–285.

Madaus, J. W., Banerjee, M., & Merchant, D. (2011). Transition to postsecondary education. In J. M. Kauffman & D. P. Hallahan (Eds.), *Handbook of special education* (pp. 571–583). New York, NY: Routledge.

Murphy, G. M., Petitpas, A. J., & Brewer, B. W. (1996). Identity foreclosure, athletic identity, and career maturity in intercollegiate athletics. *The Sports Psychologist*, 10, 239–246.

Preece, J. E., Roberts, N. L., Beecher, M. E., Rash, P. D., Shwalb, D. A., & Martinelli, E. A., Jr. (2007). Academic advisors and students with disabilities: A national survey of advisors' experiences and needs. *NACADA Journal*, 27, 57–72.

Rojewski, J. W., & Gregg, N. (2011). Career choice patterns and behaviors of work-bound youth with high incidence disabilities. *Handbook of Special Education* (pp. 584–593). New York, NY: Routledge.

Sinclair, A., & Bennett, R. A. III. (2015). The supply chain: Discourse on Black male college football players and revenue generation. In R. A. Bennett III, D. L. Graham, S. R. Hodge, & J. L. Moore III (Eds.), *Black males and intercollegiate athletics: An exploration of problems and solutions* (pp. 175–198). Bingley, England: Emerald Group Publishing Limited.

Tindal, G., Hasbrouck, J., & Jones, C. (2005). Oral reading fluency: 90 years of measurement. *Behavioral Research and Teaching Technical Report*, 33.

CHAPTER 1

IDENTIFYING AND TRANSITIONING STUDENT-ATHLETES WITH RISK LABELS AND HIGH INCIDENCE DISABILITIES

Susie C. Bruhin
University of Tennessee–Knoxville

Lori S. Robinson
Texas A&M University

ABSTRACT

The purpose of this chapter is to conceptually define the term *at-risk* as it pertains to student-athletes' academic success, to discuss commonly shared characteristics of at-risk student-athletes, and to establish a practical guide for identifying and transitioning those deemed at-risk into the collegiate environment. The authors provide a rationale for the importance of identification, communication, timing, and advocacy in supporting student-athletes who are at-risk as they transition into the collegiate setting.

The Collegiate Athlete At Risk:
Strategies for Academic Support and Success, pp. 1–19
Copyright © 2019 by Information Age Publishing

Defining *At-Risk*

Every student arrives at college equipped with his or her own unique set of academic strengths and weaknesses. However, their mastery of foundational academic knowledge and skills is essential to their continued academic success in the postsecondary setting (Conley, 2008). Basic academic proficiencies in the areas of reading, written expression, mathematics, and critical thinking are expected of all students upon arrival in the postsecondary setting, as are other foundational skills such as time management, organization, communication, and adult decision making. Most postsecondary institutions attempt to vet the aptitude of incoming students by requiring a prospective student to submit a written personal statement and participate in a live interview with a university representative or faculty member, or to achieve a set score on a standardized aptitude assessment, such as the SAT (originally called the Scholastic Aptitude Test; and later the Scholastic Assessment Test) or ACT (American College Testing). Despite the institution's hope that the process will result in an incoming cohort of students equipped for academic success, many students find themselves submerged in an environment far beyond their level of academic, social, or emotional preparedness; therefore, they find themselves in need of structure and intense academic support assistance during their transition phase (Chait & Venezia, 2009). This transition phase is critical for students who are significantly underprepared for the rigorous university curriculum, and they are often labeled at-risk for academic failure based on their previous academic resume prior to entering college.

For the purpose of this chapter, a student-athlete who is labeled *at-risk* refers to a student who (a) lacks basic academic skills, most notably in the areas of reading, written expression, mathematics, and critical thinking, and/or (b) who presents risk factors in areas such as emotional or mental health and well-being, known to impact academic success.

Knowing the Risk Factors: Common Characteristics and High Incidence Disabilities

It is a widely-held misconception that poor academic skills are the only shared characteristic of student-athletes who experience academic failure. Although scholastic abilities serve as a primary factor, socioemotional development, family and medical history, academic history, and high incidence disabilities within a family unit carry equivalent weight in assessing a student's level of risk. In addition, self-concept, educational goals, and academic motivation also serve as predictors of academic success (Simons & Van Rheenen, 2000).

Basic Academic Skills

It is not uncommon for adults to assume that the grades a student achieved in high school are an accurate picture of the student's academic skills. However, the expression "grades can be deceiving" is a common phrase in the education field and rings especially true when attempting to determine a student's true academic skills. Similarly, to the general student body, student-athletes arrive on college campuses having varied educational backgrounds; This includes those who arrive prepared with academic and transitory skills, to those whose talents or special skills, such as athletic or music abilities served as the primary focus of their postsecondary preparation. For example, in a podcast sponsored by The College Board, Earl Johnson, Associate Vice President and Dean of Admissions at The University of Tulsa, describes character as being a heavily weighted attribute admissions counselors use to evaluate a student's admission package. Johnson states that there is no formula for character; however, it includes characteristics such as leadership skills, initiative, commitment to service, a sense of social responsibility, integrity, civility, and willingness to take risks (The College Board, 2017).

Talent and character are not enough and cannot compensate for a lack in basic academic skills. The specific skills necessary for a student-athlete to be successful largely depend on the institution, the resources available, and degree program he or she is interested. At minimum, student-athletes who lack foundational skills in the following areas should be deemed at-risk and additional assessments should be conducted:

- Reading comprehension—includes vocabulary, word attack, fluency.
- Mathematics—includes fluency, basic calculating skills.
- Written expression—includes spelling, grammar.
- Critical thinking.

Socioemotional Development

The attention to the socioemotional development of students is a primary focus of many current education indicators. It seeks to focus on the holistic development of the student instead of solely focusing on the cognitive. The term *socioemotional* refers to a conception in addition to being a cognitive process, learning includes both emotional and social processes (Lopez-Mondejar & Tomas-Pastor, 2017). From a college readiness standpoint, the term socioemotional refers to solely assessing a student-athlete's cognitive abilities excludes other risk factors which stand in the way of academic success. For example, a review of a prospective student-athlete's high school transcripts will illustrate whether a lack of basic academic skills is present based upon her or his low grades. However, it frequently does not indicate factors that can impact academic performance that are seemingly unrelated to academic skills, such as anxiety, depression, or an unstable home environment.

Student-athletes who disclose information in the following (but not limited to) areas should be deemed at-risk, and additional assessments or information should be collected as soon as possible:

- Treatment or diagnosis of previous mental health issue.
- Evidence of depression, anxiety, or mood disorders.
- Experience of traumatic event or injury.
- Issues within the home environment (i.e., recent divorce, move, death).

Family and Medical History

Collecting information regarding a student's family and medical history helps identify potential risk factors, especially if suspicion of a learning disability or mental health concern is present. Since medical concerns manifest in a variety of ways, including low or declining academic performance, it is important to gather such information to help eliminate other medical issues. In addition, many learning-based disabilities are genetic in origin. Student-athletes who indicate any of the following should be considered at-risk, and further assessments or information should be collected:

- Previous treatment or diagnosis of serious illnesses or disorders for all immediate family members.
- Past serious illnesses or injuries, especially head trauma or other chronic illnesses such as sickle-cell anemia or cancer, and so forth.
- Major surgeries.

Academic History

A widely accepted practice for most academic support units for student-athletes is to compile an exhaustive report on prior academic history for each individual student. A review of a prospective student-athlete's high school transcript will indicate a potential lack of academic skills. However, it also provides the chance to identify other impactful factors. Over the past several years, student-athlete academic support practitioners have noticed an influx of incoming student-athletes who have indicated issues with learning or remembering new information (Birch et al., 2017). Additionally, many students received educational accommodations or support (through an individualized educational program [IEP] or just additional help from a teacher). Ironically, however, prior to entering college, many of those students were not previously diagnosed with a learning disability (Birch et al., 2017). This suggests that a number of student-athletes experience learning issues or receive assistance without having previously been fully evaluated by a psychologist or other licensed psychometrician professional for potential educational-impacting disorders (Birch et al., 2017).

A student-athlete presenting with any of, but not limited to, the following should be considered at-risk and additional assessments or information should be collected:

- Issues learning to read or write.
- Repeated or skipped grades.
- History of absenteeism.
- Institutions previously attended, and reasons for leaving.
- Accommodations or modifications received.
- Individualized Education Program (IEP), 504 Plan, or behavior modification plan.
- History of substance abuse.
- History of mental illness.
- History of counselling and/or therapy.

This information is helpful in determining an accurate picture of who the student-athlete actually is prior to them arriving on campus. Similarly, to college admission packets, GPA, standardized test scores, and high school transcripts only provide a small snapshot of the student. The more information an educational support unit is able to collect, the more likely the unit will be able to provide proactive strategies to aid in the student-athletes' successful transition to the institution. For example, if a student-athlete is transferring from one 4-year institution to another due to character issues, that particular student's transition plan will be vastly different from a student diagnosed with a high-incidence disability; The goal of all educational support units is to provide the appropriate individualized transition plan so the student will be successful, and thus why collecting as much information related to prior academic history before the student arrives is vastly important.

High-Incidence Disabilities

Traditionally, students who display (or have been diagnosed with) emotional and/or behavioral disorders (E/BD), learning disabilities (LD), and mild intellectual disability (MID) are classified as a student with a high-incidence disability (Gage, Lierheimer, & Goran, 2012). Most recently, Gage et al. (2012) note that students with educational impacting disabilities including, "high-functioning autism, attention-deficit hyperactivity disorder, and speech and language impairments are now being identified at higher rates" (Gage et al., 2012, p. 168), and are now classified as students with a high incidence disability, but specifically categorized as "other" within the high-incidence disabilities (Gage et al., 2012). One of the most obvious risk factors to a student-athlete's success is the presence of a high-incidence disability such as learning disabilities or speech and language impairments. The most common learning disabilities that impact student-athletes include dyslexia or dyscalculia, learning disability in the areas of reading, writing, math, concomitant with attentional issues, such as attention deficit hyperactivity disorder, known by its acronym ADHD. Other common disabilities include mental health disorders, such as bipolar disorder, anxiety, and depression, and being deaf or hard of hearing (National Collegiate Athletic Association [NCAA], 2016).

As noted previously in this chapter, many student-athletes arrive in the postsecondary setting having previously received academic accommodations or specialized support. For those who present with a prior diagnosis, proper documentation, including the student-athlete's most recent psychological evaluation, educational assessments or IEP or 504 plans administered by their previous school(s), and documentation from the diagnosing physician, should be collected. Since all students do not arrive with the proper documentation (which each institution defines and determines what constitutes as proper documentation at the university within federal American Disability Association guidelines) is determined by the institution, it is a common professional practice amongst student-athlete educational support centers that student-athletes be asked to sign a consent form authorizing their previous school(s) to release any information requested by the institution's academic support staff. If the student's documentation is outdated or does not meet the requirements for services provided by the current institution's Office of Disability Services, often the student will need to be reevaluated by a psychologist on adult scales to ensure that the diagnosis is accurate and current.

Due to recent changes in the NCAA substance abuse policy, student-athletes who indicate they are taking medications as a form of treatment for a diagnosed disorder must disclose this and provide the appropriate documentation upon arrival at the institution. Failure to disclose the use of medication or the appropriate documentation could jeopardize the student-athlete's eligibility (NCAA, 2017). Obtaining this information is extremely important, and in most if not all cases required, as it is not uncommon for students to arrive to the university wanting to continue a medication to help with attention or anxiety, especially when the student has seen success in the classroom as a result of utilizing medication (NCAA, 2017).

Self-Concept, Educational Goals, and Academic Motivation

In addition to other noncognitive factors, such as mental health and environment, a student-athlete's self-concept, educational goals, and academic motivation serve as a major predictor of his or her academic success (Simons & Van Rheenen, 2000). The demands on student-athletes to excel, not just athletically and academically, but also in maintaining a public reputation though involvement in community events, contributes to a student-athlete's thinking that athletics and academics are competing entities (Snyder, 1985). Although maintaining a balance between the two is possible, student-athletes who perceive themselves as being unprepared or incapable of achieving academic success at the collegiate level, or who do not see academic success as a primary goal pose a risk to their own success by way of creating a mindset that sees a commitment to academics as a diminishment from a commitment to athletics. This belief impacts students' motivation to succeed academically, and thus puts them at risk for academic failure. In addition, their prior home or social environment can also contribute to this belief, thus making the transition to the collegiate environment be viewed as primarily an athletic transition.

A student-athlete presenting with, but not limited to, the following must be considered at-risk:

- Diminished self-concept regarding academic success.
- Clear prioritization of athletics over academics or feeling success in both is unattainable.
- Lack of educational goals.

Taking a Team-Focused Approach to Transitioning Student-Athletes Who Are At-Risk

Student-athletes who are at-risk exist on every collegiate campus, and despite common misconceptions, transcend every sport, men's and women's (Harper & Harris, 2012). Although academic support staff play a major role in supporting the needs of student-athletes who are at-risk, other key players in this transition include coaches, parents, sports medicine staffs, and student-athletes themselves. Approaching the support of student-athletes with a team-focused tactic is an effective method for supporting the holistic and long-term development and success of student-athletes.

Five Keys to Successfully Transitioning Student-Athletes Who Are At-Risk

1. **Know the common characteristics of student-athletes at-risk.**

   Knowing what to look for is half the battle. All support personnel including academic support, coaches, athletic trainers, professors, and parents should be aware of the risk factors that affect a student-athlete's ability to succeed at the collegiate level.

2. **Conduct timely assessments of potential risk factors.**

   Not all risk factors are easy to detect; therefore, the timely assessment of potential risk factors is critical in helping to support a transitioning student-athlete secure the appropriate supports.

3. **Foster effective communication channels.**

   The African proverb, "It takes a village to raise a child" rings true when supporting the needs of a student-athlete. Parents, coaches, academic support staff, and the student-athlete themselves must communicate honestly and effectively.

4. **Promote advocacy for student-athlete support.**

   If risk factors are identified, it is important the student-athlete be empowered to advocate for him or herself. Other support staff should also feel empowered to advocate on behalf of the student-athlete to help fulfill her or his needs to achieve academic and personal success.

5. **Ongoing evaluation: Conducting timely assessments for potential risk factors.**

   One of the most critical steps in supporting student-athletes who are at-risk is identifying them as such. For many student-athletes, their academic prowess has allowed them to mask difficulties and risk factors, which continue to persist if left undisclosed. There are a number of ways to collect this information, including closely examining admission data, through conversations with the student, parental guardian, high school coaches, mentors, and so forth, during the recruiting process, and conducting screening assessments for incoming student-athletes.

The Recruitment Process

For academic support staff, the first chance to start identifying a student-athlete as potentially being at-risk is during the application and recruitment process. For academic counselors and coaches, having open conversations with prospective student-athletes helps identify risk factors early on. Examples of questions to be asked during these conversations are found in Table 1.1.

Table 1.1.
Prospective Student-Athlete Interview Questions

1.	Tell me about yourself.
2.	Why do you want to be a student-athlete at this institution?
3.	What goals do you have for yourself as a student-athlete here?
4.	Describe yourself as a student. What are your academic strengths? Weaknesses?
5.	What type of support have you received from your previous school(s)?
6.	If you have ever been diagnosed with any type of disability, such as a learning disability or ADHD, would you like to disclose that information to assist us in providing the best possible resources for you? If so, please share that information below: _____
7.	What supports do you feel you need to be successful as a student-athlete?
8.	What are your academic goals? What are your athletic goals?
9.	Who is/are your biggest supporter(s)?
10.	What motivates you to perform at your best?

Not only do these conversations serve to collect vital information and identify early risk factors, but they also help to build rapport with the prospective student-athlete. Counselors, coaches, and other support staff also have the opportunity to highlight the institution's commitment to supporting each student-athlete's unique academic needs and goals. Familiarity would suggest student-athletes experiencing some of the risk factors described previously are much more likely to disclose such if they feel the university's collaborative commitment to supporting their needs.

Conducting Baseline Assessments

Although some evidence of a student-athlete's likelihood to be at-risk is evident through information disclosed during the application process, such as high school grade point average or low ACT or SAT score, many "red flags" (i.e., warning signs) go undiscovered through this routine vetting. Even if academic skills are identified as lacking, issues such as mental health, academic and family history, and past structure are undisclosed. One of the best ways to identify these students is to establish baseline data soon after the student-athlete arrives on campus.

In order to identify such risk factors in incoming student-athletes, baseline assessments need to be administered soon after the student-athlete arrives on campus. Such evaluations will cover the major areas of risk characteristics, including:

- Prospective Student-Athlete Interview Questionnaire (see Table 1.1).
- Academic Skills Assessments.
- Academic/Medical History (see Word Table 1.2).
- Socioemotional History (see Word Table 1.4).
- Attentional Screener.

Academic support staff must select the most appropriate assessments for the specific needs of the program. Careful consideration must be made to ensure that the selected assessments are appropriate for the assessment conditions and fit within the time frame allotted.

Examples of useful assessments include:

- Nelson-Denny Reading Test (Brown, Fishco, & Hanna, 1993).
- ASRS Attentional Screener (v1.1) (see Word Table 1.3).
- Zung Depression Screener (Zung, 1965).
- Writing assessment incorporating critical thinking skills.
- Standard algebra assessment.
- Academic and family history.

At the University of Tennessee–Knoxville, incoming student-athletes are assessed prior to the start of their first semester on campus by the Learning Specialist Team housed in the educational support unit specifically for student-athletes, called the Thornton Athletics Student Life Center. This 2-hour screening process seeks to establish baseline data for all incoming student-athletes, quickly identify individual risk factors, and start the process for securing the necessary supports for each student-athlete. For some, this involves contacting the student-athlete's high school or former institution for additional documentation or scheduling an appointment for the student-athlete to meet with a licensed mental health professional or psychologist to administer further psycho-educational assessment.

Table 1.2.
Confidential Student-Athlete Screening Assessment

Name: _____   Sport:_____

Classification (circle): FR   SO   JR   SR   Transfer   DOB: _____Age: _____

I. Language & Developmental History

1. If English is not your first language/preference, what language were you schooled in? Do you have to translate back and forth between languages?

   Primary Language: _____   ☐ N/A

2. Do you have difficulty remembering or learning new information?   ☐ Y   ☐ N

3. Have you ever received Speech and Language Assessment or Therapy?   ☐ Y   ☐ N

II. Previous Academic History

4. Have you ever repeated a grade level or a course? *If yes, which grade(s) & why?* _____   ☐ Y   ☐ N
_____

5. Did you use any **accommodations (i.e., extra test time) or individual tutoring** in school? *If yes, for which courses & when?*   ☐ Y   ☐ N
_____
_____

6. Were you ever supported by an Individual Education Plan (IEP)/504 Plan?   ☐ Y   ☐ N

7. Were you ever diagnosed with a learning disability or differences? *If yes, please specify:* _____   ☐ Y   ☐ N
_____

III. Relevant Medical History

8. Do you have a family member (e.g., parent, sibling) that has had learning difficulties in school or been diagnosed with ADHD or learning disabilities? *If yes, please specify:* _____   ☐ Y   ☐ N
_____

9. Have you ever been diagnosed with Attention-Deficit/ Hyperactivity Disorder (ADD/ADHD)?   ☐ Y   ☐ N

10. Have you ever or are you currently taking any medications for the treatment of Attention-Deficit/ Hyperactivity Disorder (ADD/ADHD)? If yes, *please circle or specify: Vyvanse, Ritalin, Adderall, Concerta, Focalin,* _____   ☐ Y   ☐ N

(Table continues on next page)

Table 1.2.
(Continued)

Name: _____		Sport: _____

Classification (circle): FR   SO   JR   SR   Transfer   DOB: _____Age: _____

III. Relevant Medical History

11. Have you ever been diagnosed and/ or treated
    for emotional or mental health reasons (e.g.
    Anxiety, Depression, Traumatic experience,   □ Y   □ N
    etc.)? *If yes, please specify the reason & when:*

    _____

12. Have you ever been exposed to actual or
    threatened sexual violence, serious injury, death,
    or any other type of traumatic event? *If yes, please*   □ Y   □ N
    specify: _____

    _____

13. Have you ever harmed or attempted to harm
    yourself (i.e. cutting, burning, overdosing)? *If yes,*
    please specify when: □ Y   □ N

    _____

Table 1.3.
Adult Self Report Scale (ASRS)

Please answer the questions below, rating yourself on each of the criteria using the scale on the right side of the page. As you answer each question, place an X in the box that best describes how you have felt and conducted yourself over the past **SIX (6) MONTHS.**	Never	Rarely	Sometimes	Often	Very Often
1. How often do you have trouble wrapping up the final details of a project, once the challenging parts have been done?					
2. How often do you have difficulty getting things in order when you have to do a task that requires organization?					
3. How often do you have problems remembering appointments or obligations?					
4. When you have a task that requires a lot of thought, how often do you avoid or delay getting started?					
5. How often do you fidget or squirm with your hands or feet when you have to sit down for a long time?					
6. How often do you feel overly active when compelled to do things, like you were driven by a motor?					

Table 1.4.
Sample Socioemotional/Mental Health Screener

During the **past THREE (3) MONTHS,** how much (or how often) have you been bothered by the following problems?	**None** Not at all	**Slightly** Rare, less than two or three days in three (3) months	**Mildly** Sometimes, two or three days per month	**Moderately** Often, two or three days per week	**Severely** Nearly every day
1. Little interest or pleasure in doing things?	0	1	2	3	4
2. Feeling down, depressed, or hopeless?	0	1	2	3	4
3. So irritable that you shouted at people or started fights and/or arguments?	0	1	2	3	4
4. Thoughts raced through your head or you couldn't slow your mind down?	0	1	2	3	4
5. Much more social or outgoing than usual (i.e., telephoned friends in the middle of the night)?	0	1	2	3	4
6. Did things that were unusual for you or that other people might have thought were excessive, foolish, or risky?	0	1	2	3	4
7. Sleeping less than usual, but still had a lot of energy?	0	1	2	3	4
8. Feeling nervous, anxious, frightened, worried, or on edge?	0	1	2	3	4
9. Feeling panic or being frightened?	0	1	2	3	4
10. Avoiding situations that make you anxious?	0	1	2	3	4

(Table continues on next page)

Table 1.4.
(Continued)

During the **past THREE (3) MONTHS,** how much (or how often) have you been bothered by the following problems?	**None** Not at all	**Slightly** Rare, less than two or three days in three (3) months	**Mildly** Sometimes, two or three days per month	**Moderately** Often, two or three days per week	**Severely** Nearly every day
11. Unexplained aches and pains (i.e., nausea, rapid breathing, chest pains, trembling, pain in abdomen, neck, or head)?	0	1	2	3	4
12. Thought of harming yourself or others?	0	1	2	3	4
13. Hearing things other people couldn't hear, such as voices even when no one else was around?	0	1	2	3	4
14. Difficulty sleeping at night and feel tired, fatigued, or sleepy during the daytime?	0	1	2	3	4
15. Unpleasant thoughts, urges, or images repeatedly entered your mind?	0	1	2	3	4
16. Feeling driven to perform certain behaviors or mental acts over and over again?	0	1	2	3	4
17. Feeling detached or distant from yourself, your body, your physical surroundings, or your memories?	0	1	2	3	4
18. Not knowing who you really are or what you want out of life?	0	1	2	3	4
19. Not feeling close to other people or enjoying your relationships with them?	0	1	2	3	4

(Table continues on next page)

Table 1.4.
(Continued)

During the **past THREE (3) MONTHS,** how much (or how often) have you been bothered by the following problems?	**None** Not at all	**Slightly** Rare, less than two or three days in three (3) months	**Mildly** Sometimes, two or three days per month	**Moderately** Often, two or three days per week	**Severely** Nearly every day
20. Drinking at least four (4) drinks of any kind of alcohol in a single day?	0	1	2	3	4
21. Smoking (i.e., cigarettes, cigar, pipe, bong, e-cigarettes, vape) or using snuff or chewing tobacco?	0	1	2	3	4
22. Using any of the following medications **ON YOUR OWN** without a doctor's prescription: **painkillers** (i.e., Vicodin, Percocet), **stimulants** (i.e., Ritalin, Adderall, Vyvanse), **sedatives or tranquilizers** (i.e., sleeping pills, Nyquil, Valium), **marijuana** (including synthetic forms, such as Spice or K2), **cocaine** or crack, **club drugs** (i.e., Ecstasy/ Molly), **hallucinogens** (i.e., LSD), **heroin, inhalants or solvents** (i.e., glue), or **methamphetamines** (i.e., Speed)?	0	1	2	3	4
23. Intensely feared gaining weight or becoming fat?	0	1	2	3	4
24. Considered yourself too big/ too fat or that a part of your body was too big/too fat?	0	1	2	3	4
25. Considered yourself too small/ thin or that a part of your body was too small/thin?	0	1	2	3	4

Adapted from: Nelson-Denny Reading Test (1993); ASRS Attentional Screener (v1.1); Zung Depression Screener (1965)

Fostering Effective Communication Channels

It is the primary responsibility of the academic support staff not only to identify risk factors in incoming student-athletes, but to implement effective communication channels to help support the individual needs of those identified as being at-risk by connecting them with the appropriate services.

In an effort to best support those identified as being at-risk, examples of necessary interdependent communication entities or channels include:

- Sports medicine or team physician.
- Diagnostic psychologist.
- Student Health Center.
- Counselor or licensed therapist.
- Office of Disability Services.

Figure 1.1.   Student Centered Approach graphic.

Notice in the graphic above that all of the individual parts are centered on the student-athlete, reinforcing the commitment of support staff members working together to support the students' needs through collaborative communication and sharing of pertinent information in a timely manner.

Upon the timely scoring and review of baseline assessments, results are to be shared with the student-athlete in a confidential follow-up meeting. During this meeting, questions or concerns will be explored, additional information collected, and referrals for additional testing or support services are made.

After reviewing the results with the student-athlete, pertinent information will be shared with the student-athlete's academic counselor, athletic trainer, coach, and other members of the student-athlete's immediate support staff.

It is crucial that the channels of communication used to provide additional support to student-athletes who are at-risk are clear and confidential. Not all information disclosed is relevant or appropriate for all involved, but the student-athlete should feel the collaboration amongst the support staff. In addition, it is imperative that these pathways are established prior to conducting baseline assessments to ensure the timely review and securing of needed supports.

Promoting Advocacy for Student-Athletes Who Are At-Risk

For some incoming student-athletes, advocating for their academic needs is no novel skill. Students who arrive with prior documentation from strong academic backgrounds often exhibit strong advocacy skills and are able to effectively communicate their unique needs to all involved in their academic success. For others, especially those who arrive with undiagnosed difficulties or who come from less holistic academic environments, this process can be especially difficult. Many of these students have likely never been taught to self-advocate often because they have never truly conceptualized their disability. Accommodation and modifications have been the responses to their learning impairment, and thus self-advocacy was never intended to be a part of the equation. Because of this, the need for fellow advocates at the collegiate level is imperative. Members of the student-athlete's team should model and promote student self-advocacy by encouraging the student-athlete to better understand and communicate her or his difficulties or needs with professors or other support staff.

CONCLUSION

The level of preparedness of an incoming student-athlete and specific rigors and demands of the intended university differ greatly across the institutions comprising the NCAA. Although not explicitly stated, student-athletes presenting with risk factors and high incidence disabilities exist on every college campus, and are represented in all 23 NCAA recognized sports. Colleges and universities with athletic programs are charged with providing support to all of their student-athletes, including special accommodations for those with risk labels and high incidence disabilities, as warranted. By instituting a process by which these risk labels are identified, and additional supports or assessment is provided, colleges and universities can improve the likelihood for success for those who face significant barriers. Identification, evaluation, communication, and advocacy contribute to the success of the charge of these institutions, and create a team-focused approach to student-athlete support.

REFERENCES

Birch, L., Catanach, K., Herbst, M., Perez, J, Steinberg, M. A., & Walther, C. (2017). *Risky business: Utilization of risk assessment to optimize the learning specialist caseload*. The National Association of Academic Advisors for Athletics National Convention. Orlando, Florida.

Brown, J., Fishco, V., & Hanna, G. (1993). *Nelson-Denny reading test* [Assessment instrument]. Austin, TX: PRO-ED.

Chait, R., & Venezia, A. (2009). *Improving academic preparation for college: What we know and how state and federal policy can help*. Retrieved from https://www.americanprogress.org/wpcontent/uploads/issues/2009/01/pdf/academic_prep.pdf.

Conley, D. (2008). Rethinking college readiness. *New England Journal of Higher Education, 22*(5), 24–26.

Gage, N. A., Lierheimer, K. S., & Goran, L. G. (2012). Characteristics of students with high-incidence disabilities broadly defined. *Journal of Disability Policy Studies, 23*(3), 168–178. Retrieved from http://journals.sagepub.com/doi/pdf/10.1177/1044207311425385Harper, S. R., & Harris, F., III. (2012). *Men of color: A role for policymakers in improving the status of Black male students in higher education*. Institute for Higher Education Policy. Retrieved from http://www.ihep.org/research/publications.

Lopez-Mondejar, L., & Tomas-Pastor, L. (2017). Development of Socio-emotional skills through cooperative learning in a university environment. *Procedia–Social and Behavioral Sciences, 237*, 432–437.

National Collegiate Athletic Association. (2016). *Education-impacting disabilities*. Retrieved from http://www.ncaa.org/student-athletes/future/education-impacting-disabilities

National Collegiate Athletic Association. (2017). *Frequently asked questions about drug testing*. Retrieved from http://www.ncaa.org/health-and-safety/policy/frequently-asked-questions-about-drug-testing

Simons, H., & Van Rheenen, D. (2000). Noncognitive predicators of student athletes' academic performance. *Journal of College Reading and Learning, 30*(2), 167–181.

Snyder, E. (1985). A theoretical analysis of academic and athletic roles. *Sociology of Sport Journal,* 210–217.

The College Board. (Producer). (2017). *Character counts: What are colleges looking for?* [Episode 1]. The College Board. Podcast retrieved from https://bigfuture. collegeboard.org/get-in/applying-101/character-counts-what-are-colleges-looking-for

Zung, W. (1965). A self-rating depression scale [Assessment instrument]. *Arch Gen Psychiatry,* 63–70.

CHAPTER 2

CURRENT MODELS OF STUDENT-ATHLETE ACADEMIC SUPPORT SERVICES

Robert A. Bennett III
Denison University

Stephon Fuqua
The Ohio State University

ABSTRACT

Today academic support centers and programs have been designed to enhance the college experience of student-athletes. They are geared towards the retention and graduation of the students they engage, as well as outcomes that assist with student-athlete development (i.e., psychosocial well-being, identity development, career development, and relationship building). In this chapter, the authors explore the history and growth of academic support for student-athletes across divisions and conferences. They also examine the various models for resources available to student-athletes.

The Collegiate Athlete At Risk:
Strategies for Academic Support and Success, pp. 21–35
Copyright © 2019 by Information Age Publishing

INTRODUCTION

Gilbert Gaul (2015) noted in his book *Billion-Dollar Ball: A Journey through the Big-Money Culture of College Football*,

> An arms race has now arisen to see who can build the biggest, most lavish learning center—part of a larger, billion-dollar arms race in college athletics. So far the University of Oregon is winning, hands down. A few years back it unveiled a $42 million, three-story glass-and-steel cube called the Jaqua Academic Center, which is exclusively for athletes. The money came from Phil and Penny Knight. Phil, who once ran a 1:53 half mile for the Oregon track team, is the founder of Nike. (p. 106)

Officially called the John E. Jaqua Academic Center for Student Athletes, the University of Oregon's facility is 40,000 square feet and certainly serves as a draw for recruits. There has been much discussion around the "arms race" of college athletics, an effort by colleges and universities across the United States to have the biggest stadium, best coaches, preeminent workout facilities, an array of uniform options, and the ability to get their student-athletes to the professional ranks (e.g., National Basketball Association, Women's National Basketball Association, National Football League, Major League Baseball, etc.).

In particular, the University of Oregon has six objectives for the academic success of their student-athletes: (a) advise students with academic, social, and personal problems; (b) organize study hall for all first-year students (freshmen and transfer) with a minimum of four sessions a week; (c) monitor academic progress based on attendance and class grades; (d) provide tutoring and other means of academic help where students have needs; (e) help develop resume building and interviewing skills for the job market; and (f) support students to approach support staff with any issues. The Jaqua Academic Center has a plethora of amenities: an auditorium that seats over one-hundred people, 35 tutor rooms, 25 faculty and advising offices, a conference room, classroom space, a computer lab with over 50 computer stations, library, and lounges for students, tutors and staff. The University of Oregon's system is a grand symbol of what many colleges and universities have created to support student-athletes.

Across institutions of higher education (IHE) in the United States, the structure of academic support for student-athletes is varied. The makeup of units is based largely upon financial resources, total number of student-athletes and institutional structure which essentially are all aspects that impact human resources. As a result, model support services include personnel who can assess and treat student athletes' academic and personal needs. Without these mechanisms in place, it would be difficult for student-athletes at-risk to maximize their collegiate experience and meet

National Collegiate Athletic Association (NCAA) eligibility benchmarks and academic expectations of the institution. A historical examination of the efforts made by colleges and universities to address the academic needs of student-athletes illustrates that the structure of support services is largely dependent upon revenue, number of sports, and role of the student-athlete support office within the university structure, which often times determines allocation of resources.

THE HISTORY AND GROWTH OF ACADEMIC SUPPORT FOR STUDENT-ATHLETES

Academic support for student-athletes has its origins at The University of Texas (UT) at Austin. UT is considered the first (IHE to utilize educational staff for student-athletes (Sloan, 2005). In 1957, head football coach Darrell Royal hired Lan Hewlett, known as the "brain coach" as the first academic advisor to be associated with collegiate athletics. According to Royal's 1963 book,

> Hewlett herds our freshmen athletes through the maze of registration and indoctrination with a careful and considerate hand. He takes them in a body on orientation tours and to indoctrination lectures. He sees that they are properly familiarized with the university before classes ever start. (as cited in Sloan, 2005, p. 52)

Having a "brain coach" or academic advisor became of great importance during the 1950s and 1960s, as academic eligibility requirements were created across athletic conferences. As a result, many schools followed Royal's plan and brought in their own coaches who served as educational liaisons for student-athletes.

The current structure of academic advising with multiple staff persons who focus on class scheduling, tutoring, and managing time began in the 1970s at the University of Notre Dame (Shriberg & Brodzinski, 1984). Their structure influenced the growth of offices across the nation that included one to two people, usually assistant coaches or former coaches and players. In their roles, they were assigned the task of monitoring the academic progress of athletes (Gaston-Gayles, 2003; Gerdy, 1997). As Gaston-Gayles (2003) notes, academic support in the realm of college athletics has changed since the 1970s. In 1975, the National Association of Academic Athletic Advisors (N4A) was formed with the purpose of creating a governing body that would address the academic concerns of student-athletes (Hurley & Cunningham, 1984). Gaston-Gayles identifies the growth of academic support as a response to the changes to academic eligibility and the numerous rules created by the NCAA over the last 40 years. As a result, academic support offices have focused on "advisement, tutoring, study table, career advising, and mentoring" (Gaston-Gayles, 2003, pp. 50–51). Thus, the purpose, if not the scope, of academic support for college athletes focuses on the total development, specifically in matters outside of competition. It is more than keeping students eligible academically, or as Hawkins (2010) and Sloan (2005) note "majoring in eligibility." While academic support staff have been seen as the gatekeepers of student-athlete progress, an examination of their roles helps us determine who are the key stakeholders in the academic success of student athletes.

In 1984, *New Directions for Student Services* did a special volume focused on the experiences of student-athletes. Hurley and Cunningham (1984) poignantly assessed the dichotomy of sports and academics at the time.

> Colleges and universities have been accused of sacrificing their academic integrity in order to develop competitive athletic teams that will appear on television and draw huge crowds, producing increased revenues at a time when the traditional college-age population is shrinking. They have also been accused of compromising their moral integrity by cynically using gifted athletes for four years of athletic eligibility. The athletes then either do not graduate, or they are granted degrees even though they are appallingly illiterate and poorly equipped to handle a life without the glamour associated with athletic renown. (p. 51)

Hurley and Cunningham assessed collegiate sports at a time before the revenue athletic departments garnered totaled more than 100 million dollars annually. Yet, more than 30 years later, "academic integrity" still remains a constant topic of conversation as it relates to athletics and its role in higher education. In order to track academic data within athletics and monitor the integrity of academic support services for student-athletes, the NCAA created Academic Progress Rate[1] (APR), Graduation Success Rate[2] (GSR), and Academic Success Rate[3] (ASR). In their article, Hurley and Cunningham described an environment where academic support staff placed student-athletes in easy classes as a way to maintain their eligibility, and not necessarily benefit them intellectually or prepare them for post-baccalaureate opportunities. As a result, the foundation of academic support had to develop a model on how best to advise college athletes.

EXAMINING CURRENT MODELS OF SUPPORT

Scholars have examined the myriad of factors that play a role in the academic success of student-athletes (Comeaux & Harrison, 2011; Gaston-Gayles & Hu, 2009). However, there is not much research that explores the methods academic support staff use to ensure collegians can overcome the scholastic issues they encounter. An examination of the structure of academic support services in intercollegiate athletics reveals different models based on the structure and size of university, division of play, conference (amount of revenue generated), number of athletic teams, coaches' attitudes towards academics, as well as athletic leadership's sensibilities to educational support. For example, the National Association of Collegiate Directors of Athletics annually awards the Learfield Director's Cup to the school with the best success in intercollegiate athletics for the year. For 2016–2017, the top three schools were Stanford University (whom has finished first for 23 years in a row since the 1994–1995), followed by The Ohio State University (OSU), and the University of Florida. An examination of these schools' models for academic support helps us understand how IHE who excel in sports provide educational assistance to their student athletes.

Stanford, with 16,000 students, was ranked fifth among national universities based on the *U.S. News & World Report* (2018) best college rankings for national universities, solidifying their place as one of the premier academic institutions in the country. To support their student-athletes, they have the Athletic Academic Resource Center (AARC). Those who work in AARC "are full-time, professional staff within Undergraduate Advising and Research who partner closely with colleagues across campus to provide a comprehensive network of support that promotes a student's academic success and furthers his or her intellectual goals" (Stanford University, 2017). In all, the AARC is responsible for roughly 900 students participating in 36 intercollegiate athletic programs (15 men teams, 19 women teams, and 2 coed teams) at Stanford.

To support the holistic development of this population, Stanford has a mentoring program, the Partners for Academic Excellence. This initiative helps student-athletes deal with the transition from high school, engage in professional development, develop strategies to address athletic and academic and academic and job opportunities. First year students (freshmen and transfers) have mentors (an upperclassman and graduate student) who aid them in getting acclimated to Stanford and the academic rigors of the school, and also prepare them for job opportunities. The mentors understand the realities student-athletes face, and helps them understand how to navigate the university and life off-campus.

The Ohio State University (OSU), with its main campus located in Columbus, Ohio, has roughly 60,000 students, and was ranked 54th among national universities based on the *U.S. News & World Report* (2018) rankings for national universities. For 2016–2017, Ohio State had a record of 394 Academic All-Big Ten honorees, a league-high and school record of 115 student-athletes named Big Ten Distinguished Scholars. It was the first time OSU had more than 100 honorees. Their student-athletes are supported by the Student-Athlete Support Services Office (SASSO). This unit is housed under the Office of Enrollment Services and Undergraduate Affairs, and serves over 1,000 students participating in 36 intercollegiate sports (18 men teams and 19 women teams).

The academic accolades OSU has earned is largely due to the efforts and structure of SASSO, one of the first offices in the United States designed specifically for student-athletes. This office has 31 people whose full-time jobs are dedicated to the academic success of student-athletes. Positions include, assistant provost, senior associate director, academic counselors, and learning specialists. Each student is assigned an academic counselor who provides support for her or him on matters related to his or her academic needs, NCAA eligibility, and personal/professional development. Student-athletes are also assigned learning specialists and academic coaches who help with building academic skill. SASSO, in conjunction with the Department of Athletics also provide education abroad opportunities for student-athletes to get international education experiences. This aids in the retention and graduation of students (Student Athlete Support Services Office, 2017). One of the notable aspects of OSU's academic support is the Degree Completion Program. This effort provides scholarship for student-athletes who leave school prior to finishing their degree requirements. Students often leave early for professional sports aspirations, or family/personal reasons. As long as they are in good standing with the university (academically and financially), they are able to return and finish their baccalaureate degree at the cost of OSU.

The University of Florida in Gainesville, has 52,000 students, and was ranked 42nd among national universities based on the *U.S. News & World Report* (2018) best college rankings for national universities. Their student-athletes are supported by the Otis Hawkins Center for Academic and Personal Excellence housed under the Office of Student Life. It was built on $12.5 million, the largest donation to the athletics department at the University of Florida (Thompson, 2014). In all, the center serves roughly 650 students participating in 21 intercollegiate sports (9 men teams and 12 women teams). The school boasts to be the only Southeastern Conference school to have 100 or more student-athletes on the conference's Academic Honor Roll the last 16 years (Howard, 2017).

The University of Florida has 16 people whose full-time jobs are dedicated to the academic success of student-athletes. Positions include, senior associate athletic director, assistant director, coordinator, academic advisor, and learning specialist. They also employ course specific tutors and graduate assistants to help their students. Observing the structure of academic support for student-athletes at Florida, the academic counselors play a key role. They help student-athletes with class scheduling, tutoring, mentorship, postbaccalaureate opportunities, and any appeals processes for classes. Once students select a major they are assigned a college advisor and a counselor through the Hawkins Center. Florida claims this "double-team effort" allows many of their student-athletes to finish their bachelor degree requirements and begin a graduate program before their eligibility is finished. Florida's academic support includes mandatory study hall for first-year student-athletes as well as those at risk with a minimum of 8 hours of assistance per week. They also have individual and group study sessions, test banks, weekly tutoring, as well as interfacing with coaches. There is also a mentoring program led by graduate students and upperclassmen. Personnel are hired by the Hawkins Center to help first-year student-athletes transition to Florida.

Unique to Florida is a program that addresses student-athletes at risk, designed and operated by the University Athletic Association (UAA). In particular, the Hawkins Center has developed a comprehensive program of policies and procedures to assist student-athletes who are identified as being academically at-risk at the University of Florida. According to the university,

> During the recruiting process and orientation, the Hawkins Center gathers information on any student-athlete previously diagnosed with a learning disability or attention deficit disorder. These students are automatically referred to the Learning Specialist assigned by the Disability Resource Center to the UAA. All other incoming students are given a basic academic screening exam in order to start the process of developing an individual learning profile. (Florida Gators, 2017)

A process like this demonstrates IHE willingness to address the academic barriers student-athletes face prior to their admittance to the school. At many large institutions, the tutors and learning specialists provided by academic support staff through athletics are not available to the general student body.

Banbel and Chen (2014) note "flagship state universities not only have spent far more money for building a competitive athletic program, they usually have a far greater budget for operating an athletic academic support service" (p. 54). This means many schools, whether public or private, are unable to match the top IHE when it comes to what they can spend on athletics and the educational services that accompany this community. Banbel and Chen examined academic support in the Ohio Valley Conference (OVC), the eighth oldest athletic conference in Division I, which consists of 12 schools who average an enrollment of 10,662 students and 302 student-athletes. With these dynamics, two schools had four full-time academic support staff, four with three, five with two, and one institution with one person.

Banbel and Chen (2014) compared the numerous departments in the OVC with those from other athletic conferences. They found there were great differences in the available resources among IHE, especially with regard to the size of staff in academic support. The colleges and universities who were members of the Big South Conference averaged fewer than 5 full-time staff, members of the Colonial Athletic Association had around 7 persons, schools in the American Athletic Conference had nearly 11 staff members per department, and institutions in the Atlantic Coastal Conference averaged 14 people on staff (Simon, 2016). Simon (2016) noted the differences in size of offices "show that despite the universal challenges student-athletes face, institutions at the Big South and CAA have fewer individuals available to help student-athletes overcome these challenges and become academically successful" (p. 91). This begs the issue regarding the number of personnel in academic support. For example, an examination of non-Power 5 schools, also known as mid-majors, shows the structure of academic support is different. For example, Miami University (OH) of the Mid-American Conference (MAC) has 14 people dedicated to their student-athletes. Positions include a director, two assistant directors, a faculty rep, two academic coordinators, and eight intervention learning specialists.

Ivy League institutions treat academic services for student-athletes differently. The colleges and universities in this conference are known for having some of the highest academic standards in the United States, sports aside. On their website, The Ivy League boasts their institutions. They proclaim their schools,

> Share a tradition of academic excellence and broad-based, successful NCAA Division I athletics. The Ivy League annually finishes among the top Division I athletics conferences in national competitive rankings, and Ivy League student-athletes earn the country's best records in the NCAA Academic Performance Ratings, operating under the Ivy League model of athletics as a significant educational component of the student's undergraduate experience. Ivy student-athletes grow from their athletics experiences to become national and community leaders across the spectrum of 21st century life in business and technology, education and philanthropy, law and government, medicine and research, and professional sports and entertainment. (The Ivy League, 2017)

Like many athletic conferences, The Ivy League highlights the educational aspirations and academic strengths of its schools. The way member institutions of the Ivy League approach academic support for its student-athletes is different than how many Power 5 schools treat scholastic endeavors. For example, Harvard University in Cambridge, Massachusetts has 22,000 total students with a little less than 7,000 constituting the total number of undergraduates. From that population, there are roughly 1,200 student-athletes participating in 42 teams at Harvard. The school does not have an academic center dedicated to student-athletes. It does not provide separate academic support or have an advising center for its athletes. Their student-athletes use the same resources as all other students who attend the school. Such accommodations reflect the role of athletics in the core mission of the university, but also the expectation Ivy League schools have with regard to their students who participate in intercollegiate athletics. However, one must not mistake the high academic standards of schools such as Harvard, as not coming with high athletic demands. Ivy League student-athletes also fall subject to the "win at all cost" mentality of coaches.

The University of Pennsylvania (UPenn) in Philadelphia, also a member of The Ivy League, created the Collegiate Athletic Achievement Program (CAAP) for Scholar Athletes. This initiative exists through a partnership between The Tutoring Center and the Athletics Department. The overall purpose of this initiative is to provide tutoring for student-athletes. The academic standards do not change for student-athletes, so administrators at UPenn created this program to "assist them in balancing their academic responsibilities with the time demands of their practice schedules, travel, and tournaments" (University of Pennsylvania, 2017). Columbia University has an Enrichment Services program that caters to the academic and social development of its student-athletes. Recognizing the bulk of those who participate in varsity sports will not play at the professional ranks, the school created this initiative to ensure students have full-time employment or postbaccalaureate plans.

Within Division II, the resources do not compare to those of the major Division I schools nor schools in The Ivy League. The requirements for member institutions are different, as schools must have at least five varsity men's and women's teams. There are also fewer scholarships available at this level of play. For example, Division I schools are allowed to give the equivalent of 85 full scholarships for football, Division II schools are permitted to provide only 36 scholarships. In other sports like basketball, Division I schools can give a max of 13 scholarships, where Division II schools can only provide 10. Often these scholarships are broken up as partial scholarships coupled with other funding (i.e., academic scholarships and federal funds) to help support student-athletes. Thus, the financial revenue of an athletics department greatly impacts how schools are able support their student-athlete populations academically.

For example, Morehouse College, an all-male private historically Black college (part of a network of IHE known as HBCU[4]) in Atlanta, Georgia, is a member of Division II Southern Intercollegiate Athletic Conference and has some 2,100 students, and approximately 180 student-athletes who are involved in 7 athletic teams. Like Harvard, student-athletes at Morehouse utilize the same educational resources as the general student population. On Morehouse campus is the Frederick Douglass Academic Resource Center, which is geared to the academic success of students. All students who utilize the resource center, including first-year students (incoming freshmen and transfers), are monitored by its staff and the Athletic Academic Advisement and Enhancement Specialist. While schools such as OSU and Florida have more than 25 people dedicated to academic support, Morehouse College has less than 5. The college proclaims,

> Agency is key for our student-athletes. Failure to attend to academic matters, including attending class regularly, Crown Forum, study halls, meeting with your professors or academic advisor as required and on demand, etc., will be reported to coaches. It is the responsibility of the student-athlete to correctly sign in and out with the monitor using the scanners or sign in sheets available. (Morehouse College, 2017)

With the lack of resources, the moniker "agency is key" is important for student-athletes at Morehouse to understand. The onus is upon those who participate in baseball, basketball, cross country, football, golf, tennis, and track and field. There are no academic counselors, learning specialists, nor academic coaches from a student-athlete support office to monitor their academic progress. Personnel from the college are assigned this task, with much of the onus squarely on the student. For example, with one or two people over as many 250 student-athletes, they have to utilize campus resources and partnerships to ensure their success. As a result, a sense of responsibility is created often missing from schools with built-in safety nets for their constituents.

With schools at the Division III level, the resources are not in great abundance as seen with their Division I and II counterparts. While lesser heralded, this division has the most institutions of higher education as members. Their requirements for membership are the same as Division II schools, as they must have at least five varsity women's and men's teams. While Division I and II schools are able to provide athletic scholarships, no athletic scholarships are made available to any students participating in intercollegiate athletics at Division III schools. Thus, the financial attention to athletics also impacts the focus on academic support. Denison University, a private school in Granville, Ohio and member of Division III North Coast Athletic Conference, has a little more than 2,200 students, and approximately 180 student-athletes who are involved in 23 varsity sport teams (12 for women and 11 for men). Denison does not have a separate center for student-athletes, or staff that focuses solely on this particular population. Student-athletes at the school are able to utilize the same resources provided at the Academic Resource Center and the Writing Center. There are numerous workshops, one-on-one appointments, and special group meetings held throughout the year for student-athletes that address time management and study strategies.

When evaluating the field of academic support for college athletes, there are many unique factors to be considered. Admission requirements are often adjusted for student-athletes based on the "special talents" they possess and the institutions plan to support their success (Council, Robinson, Bennett & Moody, 2015). In all, what must be considered are the institutional policies that exist. It is the belief among many athletic councils who handle special admits[5] to their institutions where students identified as "at-risk," can achieve success in the classroom with additional academic support. An examination of the staff breakdown in academic support shows in some cases there are staff assigned specifically for football and basketball. While nonrevenue sports have personnel divided amongst other sports. There is a high turnover rate within the profession often based on many factors (e.g., salary, limitations in agency). Given the nature of working with student-athletes and coaches, it is logical to consider the possibility that pressures cause practitioners to leave the profession and even experience burn out.

There are also matters regarding credentials. Brooks, Etzel, and Ostrow (1987) illustrate many academic support staff who participated in their study had twice the experience of those working in academic support in 2016. For instance, there is a greater number of personnel who have backgrounds in psychology or sport related fields for instance sports management or administration. There are also many personnel who work across campus outside of collegiate athletics with specialized degrees in higher education. Many of these individuals worked graduate assistantships where they combined theory and practice prior to entering the field full-time. The concern in the field lies in the number of professionals who do not have backgrounds related to academic support, which is critical. This means numerous educational personnel in college athletics may not have the necessary skills to help their constituents identify the necessary skills and strategies to deal with the difficulties of school work and achieving their athletic goals. As a result, a college-athlete who is at risk academically (particularly at a large predominantly White institution) can present totally different risk factors than a traditional admit. These unique risk factors in combination with a necessity to develop agency, advocate, and build advocates supports the belief staff who work with this population need specialized training.

CONCLUSION

The history of academic support began in the 1950s as a way for coaches to acclimate and indoctrinate their players to their respective athletic programs and school. The goal then was to get young males in particular ready for the academic rigors that accompanied competition in intercollegiate sports. As the NCAA developed, conferences started to grow, and a field was established which focuses on the intellectual, academic, and social development of student-athletes. However, there is not a defined system as to how mechanisms geared towards the holistic development of student-athletes should be structured. Many of the roles and responsibilities associated with student-athlete academic support are not always clearly defined. When dealing with student-athletes who are at-risk this particular approach must be revisited especially with schools who lack the resources to properly assist their student-athletes. Research shows that at many institutions student-athlete graduation rates are comparably higher than that of the general student population at their respective institutions. However, graduation rates among men's basketball, women's basketball, and football are still significantly lower.

As it currently stands, there is great opportunity to reevaluate how institutions are serving their population of student-athletes at-risk. The standing question of if we are adequately serving the NCAA, N4A, and academic support staff needs to have greater discussions among all relevant stakeholders about how to best support the academic needs of student-athletes at-risk regardless of the academic or athletic budget of their respective IHEs. There are great disparities when the types of human, fiscal, technological and material resources available are evaluated across the different playing levels. We are mindful, nonetheless, that ample resources such as strong financial standing does not necessarily equate to better services. We embrace the notion put forth by Broughton and Neyer (2001),

> The support of well-trained staff, coaches, athletic department personnel, and the campus community is necessary for a successful and comprehensive athletic advising and counseling program. It is imperative that coaches and athletic administrators recognize the academic and personal world of the student athlete as much as they focus on the athletic arena. (p. 51)

With so many different models on how best to approach academic support for student-athletes, an ideal office setup has not been established. Although many athletic departments seek to develop comprehensive and prescriptive models that meet the individualized needs of their institutions, the lack of a universal model for academic support is problematic. In an industry that struggles with high rates of turnover (Grasgreen, 2012; Stripling, 2014), the personnel who work directly with student-athletes often work from a reactive framework where the responsibilities and duties of their position is subject to change to meet the immediate needs of any given situation. Anyone working in academic support should have mastery of the rules and regulations governing eligibility at the division, conference, and, institutional levels. This must be coupled with a comprehensive understanding of the unique nuances of the student athlete lifestyle, and how it affects the collegiate experience. The rubric for academic support, especially for students at-risk, must be based on whether professional staff are properly educated on how best to assist students and have the resources to most effectively do their jobs.

NOTES

1. Academic Progress Rate (APR) is an academic reform index set forth by the NCAA. The NCAA's APR calculation is used to evaluate team's academic progress (in place of individual athletes per se). The APR credits two points to student-athletes each academic term who meet academic eligibility standards set forth by the NCAA and its member institutions, and who remain with the institution. A team's APR is the total points earned by the team at a given point in time divided by the total points possible, which is 1,000 points (Hodge, 2015b; NCAA, 2009).
2. Graduation Success Rate (GSR). In response to criticism about its use of federal graduation rates (FGR), the NCAA established an alternative metric called the graduation success rate (GSR), which measures graduation rates at NCAA Division I-affiliated member institutions and includes student-athletes who transfer into the institution (Hodge, 2015b).
3. Academic Success Rates are reported as an indication of academic success of student-athletes for institutions with NCAA Division II affiliation. NCAA Division II member institutions report ASR. It functions the same way as the GSR for NCAA Division I institutions except ASR accounts for student-athletes that were recruited but did not receive an athletic scholarship (Blackman, 2008; Hodge, 2015a).
4. Historically Black colleges and universities (HBCU) were established in the United States of America before 1964 with the foremost mission of educating Black Americans. Today, there are some 100 HBCUs located in 19 states, the District of Columbia, and the U.S. Virgin Islands (Hodge, 2015a).
5. Special admits are students who typically do not meet an institution of higher education's standards, lessening the requirement for their admittance. This term is often applied to student-athletes who do not have the grade point average, test scores, and/or class prerequisites.

REFERENCES

Banbel, M., & Chen, S. S. (2014). Academic tutoring program and services for supporting collegiate student-athletes. *Kentucky Association of Health, Physical Education, Recreation and Dance Journal, 52*(1), 52–65. Retrieved from http://www.kahperd.com/main/Portals/0/Newsletters/JoF14.pdf

Blackman, P. C. (2008). The NCAA's academic performance program: Academic reform or academic racism? *UCLA Entertainment Law Review, 15*(2), 225–289.

Brooks, D. D., Etzel, E. F., & Ostrow, A. C. (1987). Job responsibilities and backgrounds of NCAA division I athletic advisors and counselors. *The Sport Psychologist, 1*, 200–207. Retrieved from http://journals.humankinetics.com/ AcuCustom/Sitename/Documents/DocumentItem/ 10176.pdf

Broughton, E., & Neyer, M. (2001, Spring). Advising and Counseling Student Athletes. *New Directions for Student Services, 93*, 47–53.

Comeaux, E., & Harrison, C. K. (2011). A conceptual model of academic success for student-athletes. *Educational Researcher, 40*, 5, 235–245.

Council M. R., III, Robinson, L. S., Bennett R. A., III, & Moody, P. M. (2015). Black male academic support staff: Navigating the issues with Black student-athletes. In R. A. Bennett III, S. R. Hodge., D. L. Graham, & J. L. Moore III (Eds.), *Black males and intercollegiate athletics: An exploration of problems and solutions* (pp. 69–89). London, England: Emerald Publishing.

Florida Gators. (2017). *Academic support.* Retrieved from http://floridagators.com/ sports/2015/12/10/_hawkins_center_academic_support_.aspx?path=hawkins-center

Gaston-Gayles, J. L. (2003). Advising student athletes: An examination of academic support programs with high graduation rates. *NACADA Journal, 23*(1 & 2), 50–57.

Gaston-Gayles J. L., Hu S. (2009). The influence of student engagement and sport participation on college outcomes among Division I student athletes. *Journal of Higher Education, 80*, 315–333.

Gaul, G. M. (2015). *Billion-dollar ball: A journey through the big-money culture of college football.* New York, NY: Viking Books

Gerdy, J. R. (1997). *The successful college athletic program: The new standard.* Phoenix, AZ: American Council on Education/Oryx Press.

Grasgreen, A. (2012). *Tough choices for athletes' advisers.* Retrieved from https:// www.insidehighered.com/news/2012/05/09/ncaa-academic-rules-frustrate-advisers-athletes

Hawkins, B. J. (2010). *The new plantation: Black athletes, college sports, and predominantly White NCAA institutions.* New York, NY: Palgrave MacMillan Press.

Hodge, S. R. (2015a). Black male student-athletes' academic and athletic experiences at HBCUs. In R. A., Bennett III, S. R., Hodge, D. L., Graham, & J. L. Moore III (Eds.). *Black males and intercollegiate athletics: An exploration of problems and solutions* (pp. 91–119). *Diversity in Higher Education, Vol. 16.* Bingley, England: Emerald Group Publishing Limited.

Hodge, S. R. (2015b). Black male student-athletes on predominantly White college and university campuses. In R. A., Bennett III, S. R., Hodge, D. L., Graham, & J. L. Moore III (Eds.). *Black males and intercollegiate athletics: An exploration of problems and solutions* (pp. 121–149). *Diversity in Higher Education, Vol. 16.* Bingley, England: Emerald Group Publishing Limited.

Howard, M. (2017). *Florida places 68 on SEC first-year academic honor roll.* Retrieved from http://floridagators.com/news/2017/6/28/general-florida-places-68-on-sec-first-year-academic-honor-roll.aspx

Hurley, R. B., & Cunningham, R. L. (1984, December 1). Providing academic and psychological services for the college athlete. *New Directions for Student Services, 28*, 51–58.

The Ivy League. (2017). *Prospective athlete information*. Retrieved from http://ivyleague.com/sports/2017/7/28/information-psa-index.aspx

Morehouse College. (2017). Douglass Academic Resource Center. Retrieved from http://www.morehouse.edu/academics/academicresourcecenter/studentathletesupport.html

National Collegiate Athletic Association. (2009). Defining academic reform. Retrieved from http://www.ncaa.org/

Shriberg, A., & Brodzinski, F. R. (Eds.). (1984). *Rethinking services for college athletes*. San Francisco, CA: Jossey-Bass.

Simon, R. F. (2016). *Academic support of student-athletes: A cross-conference comparison* (Unpublished master's thesis). James Madison University, Harrisonburg, Virginia.

Sloan, S. A. (2005). *The evolution of student services for athletes at selected NCAA Division I-A Institutions* (Unpublished doctoral dissertation). University of Florida, Gainesville, Florida.

Stanford University. (2017). Athletic Academic Resource Center (AARC). Retrieved from https://undergrad.stanford.edu/advising/getting-started/athletic-academic-resource-center-aarc

Stripling, J. (2014). Athletics advisers' ethical dilemma. Retrieved from http://www.chronicle.com/article/Athletics-Advisers-Ethical/149613

Student Athlete Support Services Office. (2017). Buckeye student-athletes go international 2017. Retrieved from http://www.ohiostatebuckeyes.com/sports/sasso/spec-rel/050117aaa.html

The Best Colleges in America, Ranked. (2018). *U.S. News & World Report*. Retrieved from https://www.usnews.com/best-colleges/rankings/national-liberal-arts-colleges

Thompson, E. (2014) *Gators receive record $12.5 million donation for new academic center*. Retrieved from http://www.orlandosentinel.com/sports/florida-gators/swamp-things-blog/os-gators-record-125-million-academic-center-20141219-post.html

University of Pennsylvania. (2017). Scholar Athlete Program. Retrieved from https://www.vpul.upenn.edu/tutoring/athelete.php

CHAPTER 3

DEVELOPING EFFECTIVE SELF-ADVOCACY SKILLS IN STUDENT-ATHLETES WITH DISABILITIES

Morris R. Council III
University of West Georgia

Ralph Gardner III
The Ohio State University

ABSTRACT

The purpose of this chapter is to present self-advocacy strategies as effective methods for academic support staffs to improve educational outcomes for student-athletes with disabilities. This chapter provides a rationale for why these students can benefit from self-advocacy training and explores approaches to improve student-athlete utilization of disability support services.

The Collegiate Athlete At Risk:
Strategies for Academic Support and Success, pp. 37–52
Copyright © 2019 by Information Age Publishing

Coach: *"What the hell do you mean, he's not using his accommodations?"*

Academic   *"Well coach, it is illegal to force him, and he does not seem*
Counselor: *interested in utilizing the services."*

Coach: *"The kid is struggling and needs help, so do your job and get it done!"*

This is a typical dialogue between an academic counselor and an athletic coach. Coaches are under the immense pressure to both win and ensure players' academic success. A large part of winning is making sure athletes are academically eligible. This, in turn, drives many coaches to seek any and all assistance that can keep their players from falling behind academically. Coaches view the accommodations provided by disability support services as essential to their players with disabilities academic success. In many cases, this pressure to aid the academic success of players with disabilities gets transferred to academic support staff. Unfortunately, most support staff are inadequately prepared to answer the question of why the academically struggling student-athletes are not motivated to utilize the disability services provided by the institution or how to motivate students to use these services. Although academic support staff traditionally hold strong collaborative relationships with university disability support services, these relationships alone may not be enough to engage student-athletes with disabilities in using the available services. Disabilities services are most beneficial when students realize their personal need for services and self-advocate for appropriate academic support.

Self-advocacy is an individual's ability to communicate his or her needs and desires to others (Wehmeyer, Palmer, Shogren, Williams-Diehm, & Soukop, 2013), and has been found to be a predictor of postsecondary success for students with disabilities (Test et al., 2009). Therefore, the implementation of strategies that will promote the development of self-advocacy in student-athletes with disabilities could play an important role in improving their success. This chapter examines the challenges faced by student-athletes with disabilities, describes available services for these students, and presents suggestions academic support staff can use for improving outcomes for student-athletes with disabilities. These suggestions will be presented within a conceptual framework of self-advocacy (Test, Fowler, Wood, Brewer, & Eddy, 2005).

Exploring the Problem

The Americans with Disabilities Act (ADA) defines disability as a "physical or mental impairment that limits one or more major life activities"

(Americans with Disability Act, 42 U.S.C.A § 12101 et. seq., 2008). In colleges and universities across the country, there are a growing number of college students reporting that they have a disability. According to the National Center for Educational Statistics (NCES), during the 2011–2012 year, roughly 11% of all postsecondary students reported having some form of disability (NCES, 2016). Mirroring the campus-wide demographics, there are similar percentages of students with disabilities within the student-athlete population.

Although individuals with disabilities face the same issues and challenges as their peers, their challenges are often compounded by poor social skills; significant limitations in academic skills; and/or difficulties in problem solving, decision-making, and self-management (Perry & Franklin, 2006). In the world of college athletics, these challenges are exacerbated by students' commitments to their sport. These commitments regularly isolate student-athletes, prohibiting them from having a traditional college experience. Student-athletes typically have highly structured schedules revolving around athletic practice, classes, tutoring, and games/meets.

Oftentimes student-athletes spend more than 40 hours a week on sport-related activities, in addition to their academic obligations (Comeaux, 2010). For example, student-athletes spend extensive time with training staff receiving preventative treatment or injury rehabilitation. At many universities, the time designated to intercollegiate sports participation is considered sacred, forcing student-athletes to schedule their classes around their athletic schedule, which can result in delayed graduation if all required courses do not fit around the athletic schedule. Further, the rigorous demands of their sport and classes that student-athletes navigate are often complicated by the psychological challenges associated with being a student-athlete. They must deal with internal and external pressure for athletic success, and often face uninviting academic environments (e.g., navigating negative stereotypes from faculty).

Coaches are the essential players in the development and implementation of the student-athlete schedule. Coaches are also under pressure to field winning athletic teams. The increased demand for athletic teams to compete at a high level (i.e., win) has opened the doors for unprecedented numbers of academically underprepared student-athletes with disabilities (Heydorn, 2009). This is particularly true for revenue-generating sports, such as football and basketball, because the revenue generated and other benefits provide incentive for coaches and universities to bring in the best athletic talent (Brown, 1996), sometimes inspite of athletes' prior academic performances. Universities regularly grant special allowances during the admissions process to student-athletes with academically inferior applications (Brown, 1996). These special admissions differ from nonathlete applicants with disabilities who must meet the same admission requirements as their typical peers. Many student-athletes with disabilities not only have to navigate the difficulties of their disabilities and sports, but often enter the university underprepared for the academic rigor required for college success; sometimes their performance scores on entrance exams are several standard deviations below their peers (Brown, 1996; Council, Robinson, Bennett, & Moody, 2015). The mismatch between academic skills and college course expectations places many student-athletes with disabilities at increased risk of academic failure. This mismatch may cause students to also face the stigma of being labeled "dumb jocks." This stigma, combined with an athletic culture that promotes invincibility, may influence students to hide their academic needs rather than seek disability services.

Over the years, many athletic departments have developed academic support service offices and have partnered with institutional resources to support these individuals with academic risk. These services provide ample resources but fail to explicitly educate student-athletes on how to self-advocate. In fact, providing supportive resources without teaching self-awareness and self-advocacy may foster dependency on others rather than increasing their independence. For this reason, student-athletes are at increased risk for academic failure when there is a lack of knowledge about their disabilities and how their disabilities impact academic achievement (Brinckerhoff, 1994). Assisting students with disabilities to better understand their strengths and weaknesses and to advocate for the services they need is a vital step in making them more successful in postsecondary settings and later in life. Self-advocacy is critical to the success of student-athletes with disabilities, and can be utilized to bridge the services provided by academic support offices and university disability services.

SERVICES FOR STUDENT-ATHLETES WITH DISABILITIES

Academic Support Staff

Those who work in academic support for student-athletes often face the difficult challenge of linking university academic expectations with the realities of academically underprepared students. Coaches have high expectations for academic support staff, and believe academic support staff are employed to take care of the academic needs of student-athletes, enabling students to focus on their athletic commitments (Gerdy, 1997). Although academic support services vary across institutions, their functions commonly include assisting in recruiting, monitoring academic progress, hosting transition courses, acting as liaisons with university services, tutoring, remediation, academic advising, counseling, and career assistance (Gaston-Gayles, 2003). Academic support services, are intended to provide resources to support student-athletes' through their degree programs and foster independence, however as previously mentioned often inadvertently foster student dependence. This phenomenon is critical for understanding challenges of student-athletes with disabilities because many student-athletes enter college accustomed to having decisions about their academic futures made for them by parents, high school teachers (Brinckerhoff, 1994), counselors, and sometimes coaches. Unfortunately, at many institutions, the risk of athletic ineligibility is much too high to allow student-athletes the freedom to develop decision-making skills critical to become productive adults (Gerdy, 1997). This, in turn, often places academic support staff in a contradictory space where they must decide between what is in the long-term best interest of the student-athlete and what is expedient for athletic eligibility. It is also noteworthy to mention that many support staff may feel that their job security may be directly impacted by how they address this dilemma.

Disability Support Services

Disability support services are viewed as critical tools for the success of many student-athletes with disabilities because of the documented academic benefits they yield to all students with disabilities who appropriately utilize their services (DaDeppo, 2009; Troiano, Liefeld, & Trachtenberg, 2010). The academic success of college-aged students with diagnosed disabilities varies (Clark & Parette, 2002), but should be of particular importance to those who support student athletes given their unique collegiate expereince. While services differ across institutions, the primary role of disability support offices is to provide support services (i.e., accommodations) and programs that enable equitable access to education and college life for students with disabilities. These services include, but are not limited to, assistive technology, extended time, priority registration, note-taking, and distraction-reduced space (Kurth & Mellard, 2006). Despite these resources that are designed to assist the individualized needs of students with disabilities attending college, many student-athletes decide not to utilize these services. An obstacle to student-athletes accessing disability services, is the offices are often inconveniently located on campus for student-athletes with disabilities and schedule conflicts may limit student athletes opportunities to access services. In sum, the underuse of disability services by many student athletes with disabilities may be due to the demanding schedule for athletes, a reluctance to reveal academic needs, and poor self-advocacy skills.

SELF-ADVOCACY AS A SOLUTION

By explicitly teaching self-advocacy strategies, academic support staffs can improve student-athletes' academic outcomes, and also better prepare them to be productive and independent citizens. The conceptual framework for self-advocacy (knowledge of self, knowledge of rights, communication, and leadership) as developed by Test et al. (2005) will lay a foundation for proposed solutions.

Knowledge of Self

Knowledge of self, as pertaining to persons with disabilities, has been defined as knowledge of one's own interests, preferences, strengths, weaknesses, needs, and attributes of one's disability (Test et al., 2005). Before knowledge of self can be meaningfully addressed, there must first be an established understanding that many student-athletes with disabilities have to navigate; their intellectual identity, athletic identity, home identity, and identity as a person with a diagnosed disability. For a student-athlete with a disability, prior knowledge about his or her abilities becomes a critical factor in understanding the disability.

Why is it that student-athletes do not have a better understanding of their abilities? In our society, sport is entwined in our culture and many student-athletes are celebrated at young ages for their physical abilities (Beamon, 2008) with minimal praise for intellectual achievement or development. If praise for athletic achievement is paired with lowered academic expectations by educators this can affect the way student-athletes view themselves as students and can impact their motivation for future academic advancement. In other words, student-athletes can receive explicit feedback on their athletic behaviors allowing them to grow in knowledge and skill about sport. On the hand, they do not receive the same level of feedback on their academic skills, resulting in low or no growth. Consequently, student-athletes often have a clear understanding of their athletic abilities in various situations but limited knowledge about their skills in academic environments.

Too often, student-athletes do not have adequate awareness of how their disability affects their academic and social life. Cawthon and Cole (2010) found that when examining students' knowledge of disability, many students know more about the accommodations provided to them than about their specific disability. This limited understanding can be detrimental to all students with disabilities, but particularly to student-athletes. This population in particular is least likely to encounter natural situations that allow them to address their disabilities. Social stigmas and stereotypes associated with athletic and home identities (i.e., identities that do not align with the status quo collegiate experience) often negatively influence the perceptions that peers and faculty have on an individual with disabilities.

It is critical for academic support staff to understand the concept of knowledge-of-self and the complexities that affect the student-athletes they support. This can be accomplished in several ways. Those who support student-athletes with disabilities should begin by seeking additional knowledge about disabilities and subsequently sharing that information with students with disabilities. This can be done by breaking down terminology in the student's disability assessment into plain language. Student-athletes with disabilities should also be familiar with the assessments utilized to determine the existence of a disability. The National Center for Learning Disabilities (ncld.org) is an excellent resource for gaining knowledge about high-incidence disabilities. It is important to teach individuals about their disabilities to ensure their understanding that learning disabilities are not "learning problems" or "deficits" (Brinckerhoff, 1994). Rather, by definition, a learning disability is a neurologically based, unique-to-the-individual, lifelong condition that affects the way an individual learns. One way to strongly convey this message to student-athletes with disabilities is to use positive role models. Teammates, coaches, and administrators who are comfortable disclosing their own disabilities can be videoed. The way you utilize these videos can have a range of possibilities. The videos can be privately shared between students and advisors or shown to small groups of students with similar disabilities. These videos provide a wealth of first-hand experience, and show students that they are not alone. Furthermore, they help to establish a support network for student-athletes with disabilities (i.e., "I am not alone"). Academic support staff can catalogue and organize videos and other resources by disability and create a library for student athletes to access. E-mails can also yield a variety of potential participants because they are the primary form of communication at most universities. Table 3.1 provides a sample template for support system interviews.

Knowledge of Rights

Knowledge of rights is, "knowing ones rights as a citizen, as an individual with a disability, and as a student receiving or qualifying for services under federal law" (Test et al., 2005, p. 50). College students with disabilities usually have a range of accommodations available to them through statutes such as the Americans with Disability Act (ADA) and Section 504 of the Rehabilitation Act of 1973 (Cawthon & Cole, 2010). These mandates state that schools must provide reasonable accommodations that allow an otherwise qualified student with a disability to meet required responsibilities (Section 504 of the Rehabilitation Act of 1973, 34 C.F.R. Part 104).

Table 3.1.
Support System Interview Questions

1.	State your name, professional title, and disability.
2.	How does your disability affect your everyday life?
3.	What did you do to navigate your disability?
4.	Are you available as a resource to student-athletes with disabilities?
5.	If I would have known back then what I know now, finish the sentence.

An area of concern for all students with disabilities who transition to postsecondary institutions is the shift in legislation that guides their access to disability support services (Cawthon & Cole, 2010). The Individuals with Disabilities Education Act (IDEA, 2004) is the primary statute that governs secondary schools, and it states that all students with disabilities are entitled to a free and appropriate public education (Individuals with Disabilities Edcuation Improvement Act, 20 U.S.C. § 1400, 2004). Whereas this statute requires that secondary institutions identify (i.e., Child Find) and provide services to students with disabilities. The laws that govern postsecondary institutions require the learner to self-disclose his or her disability (i.e., ADA, 504 Plan). For many student-athletes, this issue is further complicated by a fear that disclosure of their disability will negatively affect their playing time and/or scholarship. On the opposite end of the spectrum some student-athletes are passive and expect academic support staff to enforce their rights. Academic support staff must understand the law in order to advocate effectively for student-athletes and to teach them how to advocate for themselves.

Student-athletes with disabilities should first be educated that every postsecondary course will have some form of disability statement (often located in their syllabi). Students often lack knowledge of the instructional and programmatic accommodations available to them through the university. Student-athlete support staff should readily keep a handout to serve as a guide for students to view concerning how learning disabilities in reading, writing, math, and organization, can be addressed using various accommodations. Table 3.2 provides a handout for a student-athlete accommodation tips sheet. Although learning disabilities are not the only disabilities that student-athletes may have, it is the most common disability not advocated for by college students. Student-athletes must be educated that college is a privilege, and it is solely their responsibility to advocate on their behalf.

Table 3.2.
Accommodations Tip Sheet

Accommodations for Organizational Difficulties

- Contact instructor or department for a copy of the syllabus before the class begins.

  o Explicitly ask for a schedule of assignments and assessments.

- Ask for clarification during class when needed; do not suffer in silence.

- Set appointment or reoccurring appointment time with teacher for additional clarification.

Accommodations for Reading Difficulties

- Contact disability services to inquire about audio textbooks before the class begins. (Preferable after you register for the course)

- Contact disability services to inquire about additional reading services.

- Ask instructor for study guides or outlines ahead of time, so that you can focus your attention in critical information in your text.

- Ask instructor for additional time to complete reading assignment.

- Choose classes that stager reading difficulty (some intensive reading, some lighter reading).

- Participate in reading skill development workshops

- Communicate with your instructor if you are uncomfortable with speaking aloud.

- Work in area conducive to your reading habits.

Accommodations for Writing Difficulties

- Learn how to use word processors that review your grammar, spelling, and editing.

- Work ahead of the required submission time.

  o Seek proofreading assistance

- Ask instructor for alternative assignment that express knowledge in formats not hindered by written difficulty.

- Contact disability services for witting scribe prior.

- Contact disability services for note taking assistance.

- Ask professor if you can video lecture.

Accommodations for Math Difficulties

- Ask for clarification during class when needed, if unsure about symbols, or steps.

- Ask instructor for additional time to complete math assignment.

- Ask instructor for explicit examples.

- Ask instructor about tutoring services

- Utilize a calculator.

Communication

Knowledge of self and knowledge of rights only becomes transformative for learners when they can effectively communicate this information. Communication can be defined as, "effective and appropriate communication of feelings, needs, desires and an ability to say no" (Test et al., 2005, p. 50). Due to the legislation that protects post-secondary students, it becomes the student's responsibility not only to self-identify, but also question accommodations and services that may be necessary to compensate for his or her disability (Shaw, Keenan, Madaus, & Banerjee, 2010). Unfortunately, many students with disabilities, including student-athletes, do not have the skills to engage effectively in this type of self-advocacy. This is further complicated when social stigma and stereotypes influence the manner in which others interact with student-athletes. Although many college-level faculty are willing to help and accommodate students with disabilities (Cawthon & Cole, 2010; Sparks & Lovett, 2009), stereotypes associated with student-athletes, especially in revenue generating sports, has the potential to negatively affect this support (Comeaux, 2010). In addition, minority status and disability may further complicate stereotypes that negatively impact student-athletes (Council et al, 2015).

In addition to the need to communicate with disability support services and faculty, many student-athletes have a larger network of individuals (e.g., coaches, academic support staff, tutors, faculty athletic representatives) to whom they disclose their disabilities. Unlike their peers, many student-athletes are required to sign a plethora of documentation (e.g., national letter of intent, compliance forms, and often disability privacy waivers). Waivers, in conjunction with academic intake assessments and athletic department's knowledge of prior academic history, create many stakeholders with whom student-athletes must collaborate and cooperate during their educational experiences. Student-athletes with disabilities must be able to communicate their needs to coaches who might pressure them to utilize their accommodations, or place them in situations that are not conducive to their academic success. Many student-athletes with disabilities need adjustments to their athletic schedule to accommodate their academic needs, but oftentimes are unequipped to articulate this need to the necessary individuals.

Too often, student-athletes with disabilities are expected to communicate effectively with stakeholders without explicit instruction on the framework of self-advocacy. Support staffs can create templates designed to engage students in conversation about their disabilities. This dialogue can take place one-on-one with advisors or mentors, in small groups, or amongst older student-athletes with disabilities who have become leaders.

Table 3.3 provides a sample template designed to engage student-athletes in a conversation based on the framework of self-advocacy.

Table 3.3.
Student-Athlete Self-Advocacy Form

Name: _____ Support Staff _____

Describe your high school academic experience

_____
_____
_____
_____

What are your academic goals for college?

_____
_____
_____
_____

What are your career goals (if professional sports is not an option)?

_____
_____
_____
_____

Have you ever been diagnosed with a learning disability (y) (n)

If no (STOP), if yes which disability have you been diagnosed with?

Define your disability (in your own words).

_____
_____
_____
_____

Strengths

_____
_____
_____
_____

Weaknesses

_____
_____
_____
_____

(Table continues on next page)

**Table 3.3.
(Continued)**

What rights do you have as a student with disabilities?

_____

_____

_____

_____

What accommodations or modifications do you need?

_____

_____

_____

_____

Do you have a plan to address your disability?

_____

_____

_____

_____

What are the consequences for not disclosing your disability to others?

_____

_____

_____

_____

What challenges do athletic competition pose on your academic performance?

_____

_____

_____

_____

How often are you needed to communicate about your disability?

1-3 times a week   ( )

1-3 times a month   ( )

1-3 times a year   ( )

Promise Statement: I will meet with my instructor during office hours within the first week of classes to discuss my disability and goals for the course.

Review the above information with your academic support staff

Support staff can also video record a veteran professor to provide advice on expectations and how to effectively communicate with faculty (Brinckerhoff, 1994). Ideally, this instructor can be your faculty athletic representative or another qualified personnel. These videos can aid students in understanding the expectations and role that faculty members serve to students with disabilities. Finally, videos of disability support service personnel can be recorded and utilized to familiarize student-athletes with the services provided from that department.

Students should also be involved in role-play to gain experience practicing effective communication skills. This can be accomplished by utilizing a script or simply by switching roles with the student and modeling effective communication. Facilitating explicit opportunities for student-athletes to practice communicating effectively about their disability should be programed early into students' collegiate career.

Leadership

The final component of the self-advocacy framework is leadership. Leadership involves student-athletes' ability to utilize their self-advocacy skills to be change agents in and around their communities. Many student-athletes navigate their educational experience surrounded by unfair labels and stereotypes. It is the responsibility of the student to articulate his or her knowledge of self and rights in a manner that enlightens the understanding of others. By the very nature of postsecondary education, students are expected to become independent learners and citizens. Research findings indicate that learning disabilities never go away, no matter the amount of support and intervention (Troiano et al., 2010). Taking this into consideration, students with disabilities, especially student-athletes with disabilities, must strive to change the way they are perceived in academia. As student-athletes with disabilities successfully navigate their educational experience, they should be encouraged to participate in support videos and make themselves accessible to their peers with similar needs. These leaders can become the most valuable resource to academic support service offices and create a self-sustaining cycle of self-advocacy.

CONCLUSION

Student-athletes with disabilities are a unique population; they experience and manage their disabilities differently than their peers. In addition to the traditional challenges of students with disabilities, student-athletes face internal and external pressures and socially altered experiences due to their participation in collegiate sports. Many student-athletes with disabilities also enter their postsecondary institutions academically underprepared, thus placing them at extreme risk for academic failure and/or athletic ineligibility. Even under these circumstances, many student-athletes with disabilities choose not to utilize disability services, or they utilize them ineffectively. Utilizing the framework for self-advocacy, academic support staff can explicitly educate student-athletes on how to self-advocate. The academic support staff will also be better prepared to advocate for student-athletes with disabilities. The professionals who student-athletes spend the most time with outside of their coaches are their academic support staff. Academic support staff who choose not to utilize a self-advocacy framework run the risk of solely receiving student compliance based on their relationships with the student. Although these relationships are important, failing to educate students to self-advocate halts their independence and leaves them no better prepared to manage their disability.

No longer can academic support staff depend on collaborative relationships with experts across campus, because student-athlete interactions with these experts are limited. By utilizing the framework for self-advocacy, academic support services can better bridge the services provided by their department and disability support services. It is naïve to assume that students with disabilities (especially student-athletes) will self-advocate without explicit instruction in self-advocacy strategies. For academic support staff, the process of preparing students to self-advocate should begin before they ever arrive on campus. Recruiting visits and unofficial trips to campus should be utilized as formal opportunities to teach and introduce self-advocacy skills to student-athletes and their parents or guardians. Once on campus, student-athletes should be screened for academic and social risk factors and those identified as at-risk should not only receive further evaluation, but also begin strategic self-advocacy programming.

REFERENCES

Americans with Disability Act, 42 U.S.C.A § 12101 et. seq., (2008).

Beamon, K. K. (2008). " Used goods": Former African American college student-athletes' perception of exploitation by Division I universities. *The Journal of Negro Education*, 352–364.

Brinckerhoff, L. C. (1994). Developing effective self-advocacy skills in college-bound students with learning disabilities. *Intervention in School & Clinic, 29*(4), 229–237.

Brown, R. W. (1996). The revenues associated with relaxing admission standards at Division I-A colleges. *Applied Economics, 28*, 807–814. doi:10.1080/000368496328245.

Cawthon, S. W., & Cole, E. V. (2010). Postsecondary students who have a learning disability: Student perspectives on accommodations access and obstacles. *Journal of Postsecondary Education & Disability, 23*, 112–128.

Clark, M., & Parette, P. (2002). Student athletes with learning disabilities: A model for effective supports *College Student Journal, 36*, 47.

Comeaux, E. (2010). Racial differences in faculty perceptions of collegiate student-athletes' academic and post-undergraduate achievements. *Sociology of Sport Journal, 27*, 390–412.

Council M., III, Robinson, L., Bennett, R., III, & Moody, P. (2015). Black male academic support staff: Navigating the issues with Black student-athletes. In R. A. Bennett III, S. R., Hodge, D. L., Graham, & J. L. Moore III (Eds.), *Black males and intercollegiate athletics: An exploration of problems and solutions* (pp. 69–89). *Diversity in Higher Education, Vol. 16*. Bingley, England: Emerald Group Publishing Limited.

DaDeppo, L. M. W. (2009). Integration factors related to the academic success and intent to persist of college students with learning disabilities. *Learning Disabilities Research & Practice, 24*, 122–131. doi:10.1111/j.1540-5826.2009.00286.x

Gaston-Gayles, J. L. (2003). Advising student athletes: An examination of academic support programs with high graduation rates. *NACADA Journal, 23*.

Gerdy, J. R. (1997). *The successful college athletic program: The new standard.* Phoenix, AZ: Oryx Press.

Heydorn, M. (2009). Explaining the graduation gap-athletes vs. non-athletes: A study of the Big Ten and Missouri Valley Conferences. *The Park Place Economist, 17*(1), 25–33.

Individuals with Disabilities Education Improvement Act, 20 U.S.C. § 1400 (2004).

Kurth, N., & Mellard, D. (2006). Student perceptions of the accommodation process in postsecondary education. *Journal of Postsecondary Education & Disability, 19*(1), 71–84.

National Center for Education Statistics (2016). The Nation's Report Card: 2015 Mathematics and Reading at Grade 12. , Washington, DC: Institute of Education Sciences, U.S. Department of Education. Retrieved from http://www.nationsreportcard.gov/reading_math_g12_2015/

Perry, S. N., & Franklin, K. K. (2006). I'm not the gingerbread man! Exploring the experiences of college students diagnosed with ADHD. *Journal of Postsecondary Education & Disability, 19*(1), 94–109.

Section 504 of the Rehabilitation Act of 1973, 34 C.F.R. Part 104

Shaw, S. F., Keenan, W. R., Madaus, J. W., & Banerjee, M. (2010). Disability documentation, the americans with disabilities act amendments act, and the summary of performance: How are they linked? *Journal of Postsecondary Education and Disability, 22*(3), 142–150.

Sparks, R. L., & Lovett, B. J. (2009). College students with learning disability diagnoses: Who are they and how do they perform? *Journal of Learning Disabilities, 42*(6), 494–510.

Test, D. W., Fowler, C. H., Wood, W. M., Brewer, D. M., & Eddy, S. (2005). A conceptual framework of self-advocacy for students with disabilities. *Remedial and Special Education, 26*, 43–54.

Test, D. W., Mazzotti, V., Mustian, A., Fowler, C., Kortering, L., & Kohler, P. (2009). Evidence-based secondary transition predictors for improving post-school outcomes for students with disabilities. *Career Development for Exceptional Individuals, 32,* 160–181.

Troiano, P. F., Liefeld, J. A., & Trachtenberg, J. V. (2010). Academic support and college success for postsecondary students with learning disabilities. *Journal of College Reading and Learning, 40,* 35–44.

Wehmeyer, M. L., Palmer, S., Shogren, K., Williams-Diehm, K., & Soukup, J. (2013). Establishing a causal relationship between interventions to promote self-determination and enhanced student self-determination. *Journal of Special Education, 46,* 195–210.

CHAPTER 4

MEASURING ACADEMIC SUCCESS

How the Standardization of Evaluating Academic Achievement Leaves Students At-Risk Behind

Emily M. Newell
University of Southern Maine

Morris R. Council III
University of West Georgia

ABSTRACT

In this chapter, the authors provide an overview of how schools measure academic success, with a focus on the NCAA and other intercollegiate governing bodies (e.g., NAIA, NJCAA). They also discuss the frustration between contingencies required to promote eligibility and the belief that those contingencies alone fail to promote a positive educational experience. Finally, the authors examine if traditional assessments are meaningful enough to capture the progress of student athletes who are at risk academically. Recommendations are provided for improved evaluation of student success and success of support offices.

The Collegiate Athlete At Risk:
Strategies for Academic Support and Success, pp. 53–76
Copyright © 2019 by Information Age Publishing

"But at times, pressures from coaches to keep athletes eligible—sometimes at the expense of an athlete's academic pursuits—were too much to bear. So much so that after 20 years in the business, she recently left it. 'It just—it gets to be a lot,' she says. 'You can feel the walls closing in on you, from all sides.' " (Grasgreen, 2012b)

Many academic counselors have experienced moments of frustration. Whether in a call or e-mail from a coach about a prospective student-athlete who does not meet the academic standards of the institution, or during the struggle of attempting to help student-athletes balance a course load that works with their practice schedule, meets university and program requirements, and also meets National Collegiate Athletic Association (NCAA) standards for academic progress, meeting the standardized measurements of student-athlete "academic success" can be overwhelming. Academic standards for initial and continuing eligibility set by governing bodies like the NCAA, the National Association of Intercollegiate Athletics (NAIA), the National Junior College Athletic Association (NJCAA), among others, can make academic coordinators working with student-athletes question their purpose of helping student-athletes become and remain academically successful. Many find themselves doing just enough to help student-athletes remain active on the team roster (Grasgreen, 2012a, 2012b; Wolverton, 2015).

The debate over the quality of student-athletes admitted to colleges and universities, and on the education provided to those student-athletes, has been under close examination for decades. As early as the 1970s and 1980s, research has shown student-athletes are frequently admitted to colleges and universities with much lower GPA and SAT results than the general student body population (Brown, 1996; Gurney, 2011; Purdy, Eitzen, & Hufnagel, 1982). Even the NCAA—the most prominent national governing body for college athletics—has minimal rules regarding academic standards. According to the most recent NCAA Division I rulebook, colleges and universities are permitted to admit student-athletes they can "reasonably expect" to obtain a degree (NCAA, 2016). NCAA Division II schools abide by the same policy as Division I, while the NCAA Division III rules state admitted students must meet the academic standards for admission set by the institution. The NAIA and NJCAA each have their own academic standards required of student-athletes to be admitted to college, and to remain eligible for play, ranging from simply graduating from an accredited high school to obtaining specific grade point average (GPA) and standardized test scores to being enrolled and passing a certain number of credit hours each term (NAIA, 2016; NJCAA, 2016).

When working with student-athletes with disabilities, the obstacles to eligibility only increase. Initial eligibility weighs heavily on high school GPA and standardized test scores, both of which can be significantly impacted by students with diagnosed, and especially undiagnosed, learning disabilities. For students who did not have the resources during the course of their K–12 education, college may be the first time they become aware of the learning disabilities that were barriers to greater academic success. Additionally, students who underperformed in the areas of math and English in high school are often required to take remedial coursework upon their arrival on campus. These courses may or may not count toward their continuing eligibility, depending upon the type of institution they attend (e.g., NCAA, NAIA, or NJCAA member schools). Athletic academic counselors must be mindful of the academic profile of student-athletes, and how the courses required of them impact their eligibility. At times, support staff push student-athletes toward specific courses and degree programs based on how the requirements fit with their high school academic profile. This type of action reflects the availability of remedial course requirements that exist as a means to help keep the student eligible for the entirety of his or her time at the institution.

This multifaceted tug-of-war between student-athlete remedial requirements, academic and career interests, and eligibility can cause great tension between the athletic academic counselor, coach, and student-athlete, as each attempt to look out for a certain special interest. In this chapter, the authors provide an overview of the initial and continuing eligibility standards for the three-primary intercollegiate athletic governing bodies—the NCAA, NAIA, and NJCAA. They also discuss how particular measures are used to evaluate the academic success of student-athletes and the overall success of the academic support offices overseeing student-athletes' academic progress. Furthermore, the authors critically evaluate whether these measurements are truly indicative of academic success, especially for those at risk academically. Finally, the authors assess the broad impact these regulations and evaluation standards have on all involved parties, including the student-athletes and academic counselors. There will be a particular focus on academic counselor burnout and motivation, before providing a course of action for better evaluation of individual student-athlete and academic office academic success.

Eligibility and Measures of Academic Success

One of the trending concerns in the world of student-athlete academic support is the growth of major NCAA enforcement cases, including notable cases at the University of North Carolina at Chapel Hill and Syracuse. These particular situations had athletic academic support staff members at the center of a controversy. In a 2016 *Inside Higher Ed* article, it was reported academic misconduct had occurred at Division I institutions more than a half dozen times since 2014, and noted the NCAA commented it was investigating another 20 similar cases (New, 2016). The same report indicated over the course of the past 2 decades, NCAA Division I institutions have been penalized for academic fraud at least 15 times. A quick look through the NCAA's legislative database shows when expanded to include Divisions I, II, and III, the number of NCAA enforcement cases involving academic misconduct, jumps to more than 90 since 2000.

So why the rise in academic misconduct cases over the past 2 decades? Critics have argued while the NCAA sees itself as well-intentioned in increasing academic standards, first with the 2003 academic reform package that introduced academic progress rate (APR) as a measure of academic success, followed by 2011 reforms that held schools to higher standards for team academic performance, those reforms have hurt rather than helped student-athletes. Most notably, such reforms prevented the University of Connecticut Men's Basketball Team from competing in the 2012 NCAA Men's Basketball Championship tournament due to its 5-year APR score falling below the standard the governing body deemed acceptable. Again, critics were pointed to the standard unmet by the team, and decried it as punishing a current team for a less than 50% graduation rate maintained by student-athletes who left the institution. New academic standards introduced in 2016 would now make any breach of university or college academic integrity policies a violation of the NCAA academic misconduct policies. Redefining the existing impermissible academic benefit violation rule to include those professionals—including athletic staff members or boosters—would provide a benefit outside of the purview of university or college academic integrity policies (New, 2016).

This ever-increasing policing and scrutiny of academic misconduct and academic success of intercollegiate athletics programs is likely to only continue to put more and more pressure on the athletic counselors and other academic practitioners who work with student-athletes to assist student-athletes in remaining eligible while still avoiding the increasingly murky waters of academic misconduct and academic fraud. With pressure from coaches, student-athlete eligibility, and potential NCAA investigations at hand, the mounting pressure this puts on practitioners can lead to high burnout, all while not proving to actually provide student-athletes with an academically successful experience, particularly those who struggle with learning disabilities.

NCAA Eligibility

"Our unit does not advise based on how to keep students eligible, which this legislation is encouraging," one adviser said. "We will continue to encourage students to excel in the classroom; however, more emphasis will now have to be placed on eligibility, as opposed to academic excellence. We can now, officially, be classified as 'eligibility brokers' instead of 'academic advisers.' " (Grasgreen, 2012b, para. 35)

Since 2004, the NCAA has made increasing efforts to monitor and regulate the academic performance of student-athletes both individually and as teams, while attempting to push student-athletes to higher achievement levels through an initial academic reform package and numerous updates. These regulations include rules regarding minimum credit hours of enrollment per semester, minimum credit hours passed per semester (for which an increased standard of 9 fall semester hours was introduced and required for all football student-athletes beginning in 2011), minimum GPA requirements, and degree progress requirements individually and as a team. However, critics of the rules argue the reform forces student-athletes to decide between eligibility and interests. As a result, practitioners that work with this population are influenced to do the same (Wolverton, 2014). At the most critical level, it has been said the rules put into place by the NCAA to regulate student-athlete academics "wrongly assume that an athlete who graduates received a good education" (Grasgreen, 2012b, para. 3).

Academic Progress Rate (APR)

At the team level, the NCAA implemented an additional index in an effort to ensure academic integrity in 2004. Its academic progress rate (APR) measurement system was employed as a way of keeping its member schools accountable for the education of their student-athletes (Hamilton, 2005). According to the NCAA,

Each student-athlete receiving athletically related financial aid earns one point for staying in school and one point for being academically eligible. A team's total points are divided by points possible and multiplied by 1,000 to produce the team's APR. A 930 APR predicts about a 50 percent graduation rate. (NCAA, 2014b, paras. 4–5)

In the 2012–13 competition season, the NCAA began banning teams who fell below a 930 multiyear APR score (calculated as the average over a 4-year period) from postseason and championship competition, thus increasing the importance of student-athlete eligibility and retention.

All of this was done in an effort to curb criticism college athletics was exploitative (i.e., student-athletes as an unpaid labor force), a mere minor league system for U.S. professional sports organizations. The NCAA reported since the introduction of APR as an index for academic success, 4 year average APR scores have continued to rise in a number of sports, noting the increases to average scores about 950 for the sports of football, baseball, and men's and women's basketball (Hosick, 2011). However, even with penalties for lackluster academics in place, teams at the highest level of competition continue to fall short in graduating their student-athletes. As previously explained, a score of 930 indicates a graduation rate around 50%. It should be noted not all student-athletes or athletic teams struggle to maintain high graduation and retention rates. Football programs at Clemson University, Northwestern University, Stanford University, the University of Michigan, The Ohio State University, and the University of Wisconsin–Madison makeup a group of several programs who have been recognized consistently over the past decade for having APR scores in the top 10% of all college football programs (NCAA, 2016a). Both male and female student-athletes are often admitted to colleges and universities underprepared. However, a vast majority of student-athletes at risk for academic failure and teams with low APR rates are clustered into the sports of men's basketball and football at the Division I level (Winters & Gurney, 2012).

Despite the level of practitioner frustration with these academic require- ments, there are reports of positive impacts of the NCAA reform package that created APR and has subsequently increased penalties for teams that have repeatedly low APR scores. NCAA reported statistics showed in the 10 years following the implementation of APR as a measure of academic success for student-athletes in a team setting, the number of student-ath- letes who depart their institution of enrollment decreased by more than 40 percent. In addition, the NCAA has since allowed schools an "earn back" system of sorts, where student-athletes who depart prior to gradua- tion—meaning the team on which they completely lost at least one point for retention, and possibly another for departing the institution academi- cally ineligible—can re-enroll at the college or university later, and, after earning their degree, earn their retention point back. Again, NCAA statis- tics reported since 2004, nearly 13,000 student-athletes have re-enrolled and earned their degrees (Hosick, 2011).

When the NCAA decided to raise minimum APR scores required for participation without penalty from 900 to 930 in 2011 (which became the minimum for this level starting with the 2014–15 academic year), it implemented a three-level penalty structure that increases as schools receive multiple academic penalties (Hosick, 2011). Aside from a postsea- son ban—implemented after a school posts a sub-930 one-year or sub-940 two-year average APR score—teams begin at the first level and move up each sequential year the team continuously fails to reach the benchmark of 930. The penalties are outlined in Table 4.1.

Table 4.1.
NCAA Division I APR Penalty Structure

Penalty Level	Description of Penalties
Level 1	Penalties focus on practice restrictions, allowing teams to use that time to focus on academics. Teams facing this penalty lose four hours and one day of practice time per week in season, replaced with academic activities.
Level 2	Penalties include the Level One penalty and a reduction of four hours of practice time out of season replaced with academic activities. This level also includes the elimination of the non-championship season or spring football. Teams without non-championship seasons face a reduced number of contests.
Level 3	Penalties include all Level One and Two penalties, plus a menu of potential additional penalties. These can include financial aid reductions; additional practice and contest restrictions, coach-specific penalties (including game and recruiting restrictions); restricted access to practice for incoming students who fall below certain academic standards; restricted membership; and potential multi-year bans on postseason competition.

Source: http://www.ncaa.org/about/resources/media-center/news/student-athletes-continue-achieve-academically

In the 2014–15 academic year, 36 NCAA Division I teams were ineligible for postseason competition, and 57 faced additional penalties based on the level-specific penalties outlined in Table 4.1. Why does APR matter beyond postseason competition and practice hours? Does APR truly promote the advancement of skills practitioners who bridge the gap between academics and athletics see as actual academic achievement and success? The NCAA has continued to reinforce APR was created utilizing the variables student-athlete retention and student-athlete eligibility, the organization reaffirms, because retention and eligibility are the greatest predictors of persistence and eventual graduation by student-athletes (Hamilton, 2005). A set of issues raised by Singleton (2013) questions the lack of viable data as to whether an APR score of 930 actually translates to a graduation rate of 50%. In fact, information collected from a study she conducted using publicly available graduation rates and APR scores indicated more than 100 Division I men's basketball, women's basketball, and football programs had federal graduation rates above 50% and APR scores below the then standard 925, or APR scores above the then-standard APR above 925, and federal graduation rates below 50%.

A study completed fairly early into the implementation of APR as a measurement of academic success by Christy, Seifried, and Pastore (2008) attempted to gauge athletic administrators' perspectives on the impact of APR on student-athletes, teams, and programs. The respondents included

47 administrators and 28 head coaches ($n = 75$) from schools competing within the NCAA Division 1 Bowl Championship Subdivision (BCS). While a majority ($n = 48$) of the administrators surveyed believed APR would have a positive effect on student-athletes, 32% ($n = 24$) believed the implementation of APR requirements would have little to no impact on student-athlete academic performance.

Progress Toward Degree (PTD)

"In Evans's experience, an at-risk athlete who has just floated along to maintain eligibility has few choices when it comes time to choose a major. A college GPA that's hovering around 2.0 doesn't allow for many options" (Grasgreen, 2012b, para. 16). Progress Toward Degree (PTD) is the NCAA calculation introduced in the 2003 reform package to help fight what at the time were dwindling graduation rates. PTD is a percentage calculation based on the number of credit hours a student-athlete has taken that directly apply to the degree program in which the student is enrolled (and can include general education credit hours required by the program) divided by the total number of degree hours required to graduate from the degree program of enrollment. The "40-60-80 Rule" as it is often called, means by the end of a student-athlete's second year of enrollment, he or she must have completed at least 40% of the degree-specific hours required by his or her program. It increases to 60% by the end of the student-athlete's third year, and to 80% by the end of the fourth year. Such a formula is designed to keep student-athletes on track to graduate in 5 years (NCAA, 2014b).

Some provisions to the NCAA PTD requirements and enrollment minimums are made for student-athletes with learning disabilities. First, the NCAA does provide a process of submitting waivers available to student-athletes who miss one of these benchmarks, but the granting of a submitted waiver is not guaranteed. The complete language of the waiver rule for less than full-time enrollment (FTE) is shown in Figure 4.1.

NCAA bylaw regarding PTD waivers for students with learning disabilities

14.2.3.4 Student-Athletes With Education-Impacting Disabilities. The Progress-Toward-Degree Waivers Committee (see Bylaw 21.7.5.1.3.2) may waive the 12-hour requirement for a student-athlete when objective evidence demonstrates that an institution defines full-time enrollment for that student-athlete to be less than 12 hours to accommodate for the education-impacting disability. *(Adopted: 1/10/95, Revised: 11/1/07 effective 8/1/08, 8/7/08, 1/16/10 effective 5/1/10)*

Source: 2016–17 NCAA Division I Rules Manual (NCAA, 2016b).

Figure 4.1.   NCAA bylaw regarding PTD waivers for students with learning disabilities.

There are also provisions made where some remedial coursework can be counted toward a student-athlete's PTD and term enrollment minimum calculations, but the amount of remedial coursework counted is limited. Outlined fully in Figure 4.2, the NCAA provides room within the FTE regulations and PTD calculation for the consideration of remedial coursework, but those classes must meet several requirements.

NCAA bylaw regarding how remedial courses count toward eligibility

14.4.3.5.4 Remedial, Tutorial or Noncredit Courses. Remedial, tutorial or noncredit courses may be used by the student to satisfy the minimum academic progress requirement of Bylaw 14.4.3.1 only if they meet all of the following conditions: *(Revised: 10/31/02 effective 8/1/03)*

    (a) The courses must be considered by the institution to be prerequisites for specific courses acceptable for any degree program;

    (b) The courses must be given the same weight as others in the institution in determining the student's status for full-time enrollment;

    (c) Noncredit courses may not exceed the maximum institutional limit for such courses in any baccalaureate degree program (or the student's specific baccalaureate degree program once a program has been designated); and

    (d) Credit in such courses shall not exceed six-semester or nine-quarter hours, and the courses must be taken during the student's first academic year of collegiate enrollment.

Source: 2016-17 NCAA Division I Rules Manual (NCAA, 2016b).

Figure 4.2. NCAA bylaw regarding how remedial courses count toward eligibility.

First, remedial coursework is deemed as such by the credit-granting institution. Second, a student-athlete may only count remedial coursework as credit toward FTE and PTD requirements if the course is considered a prerequisite to a course for her or his degree program. Thus, students cannot choose to take a lower-level class if the subsequent course is not required to complete their degree. Finally, student-athletes requiring coursework for their degree program can only count those credit hours toward FTE during their first year of collegiate enrollment. As a result, the student-athlete can only count 6 total credit hours toward the FTE and PTD calculations. Therefore, those who enter college requiring more than 6 hours of remedial coursework in order to obtain a degree must still enroll in the required hours for eligibility, but only the first 6 hours of remedial courses taken may be counted.

For example, if John Student needs 9 hours of remedial math coursework in order to take the regular required math course for his degree program, he must still take all 9 remedial hours, but only 6 of them will count. This means he must make up the additional 3 hours in regular coursework to meet the minimum FTE requirements and PTD require-ments. Because a student must past 24 credit hours prior to the start of his or her second year, if one is required to take 9 hours of remedial math, she or he must actually take 27 credit hours to account for the 3 hours of math that will not count toward the NCAA requirements. It is quite a daunting task for practitioners to explain to student-athletes the need to take additional coursework when they student-athletes are struggling to pass their respective courses in which they are enrolled. These rules only put additional pressure on student-athletes that may be already struggling to balance athletics and academics.

Similar to APR, PTD has come under criticism from practitioners and media critics for promoting eligibility over actual learning, and prevent-ing student-athletes from pursuing degrees in the program of their choice. A major criticism of the use of PTD to measure the academic success of student-athletes came from the Knight Commission on Intercollegiate Ath-letics. They argued student-athletes would be more apt to enroll in "easy" majors, leading to an increase in clustering (i.e., the enrollment of a dispro-portionately high number of student-athletes in a specific degree program when compared to the overall student body enrollment in that program) if schools measured degree percentages based on a singular program. Thus, student-athletes were "stuck" in their major of initial enrollment, as transferring to another could significantly hamper their PTD calculation, causing academic ineligibility (Wolverton, 2015).

This sentiment was echoed by the National Association of Academic Advisors for Athletes (N4A), which issued a public letter and report in which the then-president of the organization criticized the implementation of PTD, fearing student-athletes and advisors would feel continuous pres-sure to ensure student-athletes are enrolled in degree programs that allow them to easily meet eligibility requirements at a given moment as opposed to a degree program they would prefer, or they desire (National Association of Academic Advisors for Athletics, 2004).

The argument continues to be whether PTD allows for student-ath-letes to freely choose an academic major, and what pressure this puts on academic counselor student-athletes may seek guidance feel pressure to ensure student-athletes enroll in majors they feel completely confident the student would be successful in, or programs with lesser hour requirements.

It should be noted while there are many criticisms of the NCAA PTD model of calculating the continuing eligibility of student-athletes, there are some positives. The "40-60-80" model does have good intentions in keeping student-athletes on track to obtain their degrees in 5 years. As athletic academic professionals, the goal is to promote student learning without feeling pressured to push a student-athlete into any specific degree program for the purpose of athletic eligibility. However, that is an arduous task to ask of athletic academic practitioners. The quotes from industry professionals and information presented throughout this chapter illustrate the immense pressure they feel, whether it is from coaches to ensure student-athletes' eligibility, or the pressure they witness student-athletes bearing when selecting a major. Although these rules were put in place for the purpose of promoting student-athlete persistence and graduation, practitioners argue this has not been the case (Grasgreen, 2012a, 2012b).

Graduation Success Rates (GSR) and Academic Success Rates (ASR)

The NCAA Graduation Success Rate (GSR) measurement, utilized to distinguish the difference between student-athlete retention and graduation rates reported federally at the Division I level, takes into consideration transfer student-athletes who leave in good academic standing for professional careers (NCAA, 2014a). Both federal graduation rates and GSR are calculated utilizing a 6-year track for graduation. For student-athletes who transfer in good academic standing from their first school to another institution (i.e., they are eligible for competition), the GSR does not count against the latter institution. The Academic Success Rate (ASR) is similar, but is utilized at the NCAA Division II and III levels. It includes all participating student-athletes, not just those on athletic scholarships, which is what GSR uses at the Division I level.

This method of counting "graduating" student-athletes neglects any follow up. It also fails to take into account a student-athlete who may transfer to another school, become academically ineligible, or depart the institution prior to graduation without enrolling elsewhere. In these cases, only student-athletes who receive athletic scholarships are used in the graduation rate calculation. Therefore, student-athletes not on athletic scholarships, for which athletic academic counselors are still responsible, are not used for calculation in these rates. This can lead to a lack of interest from coaches in how these student-athletes perform academically. Such an approach leaves academic counselors in a dilemma. They must consider how much time and resources are dedicated to student-athletes who are not on scholarship, but require academic accommodations due to learning disabilities.

As addressed at the beginning of this chapter, the pressure to ensure student-athletes are eligible for competition felt by academic practitioners is increased for students-athletes who will impact GSR or APR scores of teams. Later in this chapter, we analyze the overload and burnout experienced by these practitioners who fall under pressure for students to remain academically eligible, maintain high eligibility and graduation rates of scholarship students, and still provide quality assistance to all students.

National Association of Intercollegiate Athletics (NAIA)

The NAIA has academic eligibility standards that dictate a prospective student-athlete's ability to initially be eligible for competition. In comparison, the NAIA's rules are less stringent than the recently increased NCAA requirements. Students under the NAIA are eligible when they meet two of the three following standards: (1) achieve a minimum test score on either the SAT (940); or ACT (composite score of 18), (2) graduate from an accredited high school with at least a 2.0 GPA on a 4.0 scale; and (3) graduate in the top half of the student's high school class (NAIA Clearinghouse, 2018).

For continuing eligibility, there are two to four main rules that must be met by all student-athletes enrolled at an NAIA institution. First, all student-athletes must be enrolled in 12 institutional credit hours per semester. Freshmen who wish to remain eligible after their first semester of enrollment must pass 9 of the 12 credit hours in which they are enrolled (regardless if the first term of enrollment is fall or spring). After the first two semesters of enrollment (during which the 12 credit hours of enrollment and 9 hours passed rules are in effect), student-athletes must adhere to the 24/36-hour rule, which is similar to the NCAA PTD rules, that requires student-athletes to have completed 24 semester hours or 36 quarter hours.

Also like the NCAA, the NAIA has a degree progress rule that is similar to that of the 40-60-80 PTD requirement. However, rather than basing it on the student-athlete's progress in his or her individual degree program, the NAIA requirements are based solely on credit hours. Student-athletes must have accumulated 24 semester hours or 36 quarter hours prior to the beginning of their second season, 48 semester or 72 quarter hours prior to their third season, and 72 semester or 108 quarter hours prior to their fourth season. Additionally, by the time the student-athlete reaches year four, 48 of the 72 hours completed must meet general education or degree-specific requirements for the program in which the student-athlete is enrolled. During their final 2 years (years 3 and 4), the student-athlete must also maintain a 2.0 cumulative GPA in order to maintain playing eligibility during those seasons.

What is of interest is the NAIA's permission to grant a learning disability exception for prospective student-athletes who are identified as having been on an individualized education program (IEP) during high school (NAIA Eligibility Basics). An IEP is a legally binding document containing individualized written statements of services designed to address the needs of K–12 students with diagnosed disabilities. Prospective student-athletes who would like to apply for a learning disability exception to the standardized NAIA initial eligibility rules includes the student providing an official diagnosis from a doctor, a copy of the student's IEP or 504 plan where applicable, standardized test results along with subsection scores, a statement of accommodations the institution of desired enrollment commits to making for the student individualized to fit the prospective student-athlete's specific disability and needs, and all previous transcripts. While permissions are granted for initial eligibility waivers for students with learning disabilities, it should be noted the NAIA rulebook, unlike those of the NCAA and NJCAA, does not make any mention of remedial coursework, and how that may be counted toward a student-athlete's academic progress. Additionally, unlike the NCAA, the NAIA does not explicitly outline its waiver process for not meeting degree progress specifically because a student-athlete has been identified as having a learning disability. It does note student-athletes with documented learning disabilities have the opportunity to appeal ineligibility due to academic progress because of his or her learning disability.

Although slightly less stringent than the NCAA academic standards (which, it should be noted, have increased substantially since 2003), the degree progress and GPA requirements required by the NAIA is structured similarly, and therefore places onus on academic professionals working with student-athletes to help ensure those student-athletes continue to meet these benchmarks, which some advisors have noted are well below what many degree programs expect (Grasgreen, 2012b). This can lead to student-athletes limiting potential major choices, as the focus shifts not from obtaining the needed GPA for admission to the most academic degree programs, but instead simply remaining eligible academically for athletic competition. While the NAIA comes under less scrutiny publicly and in major media, its degree progress measures closely mirror those by the NCAA. Thus, it could be inferred if the same level of scrutiny was applied to these programs, critics would argue defining success by hours applied directly to a singular degree program can be detrimental.

National Junior College Athletic Association (NJCAA)

The last major organization evaluated in this chapter in terms of eligibility and academic assessment is the National Junior College Athletic Association (NJCAA). Like the NCAA and NAIA, the NJCAA has initial and continuing eligibility requirements that student-athletes must meet in order to be eligible for competition. The least rigorous of the three athletic divisions, the NJCAA only requires prospective student-athletes "be a graduate of a high school with a state department of education approved standard academic diploma, state department approved general education diploma, or a state department of education approved high school equivalency test" (NJCAA, 2016, p. 1). In addition, all student-athletes must be enrolled full-time at the institution of competition by the 15th day of the academic term or they will be ruled ineligible. As a result, student-athletes who enroll after the 15th day are disqualified from participating athletically.

The NJCAA has continuing eligibility rules student-athletes must meet in order to remain eligible for play. Although in cases where student-athletes intend to transfer to a 4-year college or university, student-athletes must remain above the NJCAA minimums. After the first year of participation, student-athletes competing at NJCAA member schools must meet the same academic standards as those attending NAIA schools: at least 24 semester hours or 36 quarter hours. In addition, the student must have achieved at least a 2.0 GPA. As the NJCAA is made up of community/junior colleges, student-athletes will only compete for 2 years of enrollment as an eligible student-athlete.

Of note in the NJCAA eligibility rules in regard to student-athletes tagged at-risk or those with a learning disability is the organization's rules regarding remedial coursework. Not only does the NJCAA allow remedial coursework to count toward a student-athlete's FTE status, but it allows an unlimited number of remedial hours to count, unlike the very stringent NCAA rules (NJCAA, 2016). The NJCAA makes extensive mention of student-athletes with learning disabilities in its rules manual, as shown in full in Figure 4.3. Although the NCAA requires a specific waiver, the NJCAA lets the institution determine if a decreased course load is the correct course of action for a student-athlete with a learning disability. This allows the student-athlete to enroll in 6 to 11 hours per semester and be considered to be meeting FTE requirements. The institution, based on its individual evaluation of the student-athlete's specific learning needs, determines the number of credit hours of enrollment required by the student-athlete with a documented learning disability.

IMPLICATIONS OF STANDARDIZED MEASURES OF ACADEMIC SUCCESS

Many of the young professionals are former student-athletes who earn a master's degree in something related to counseling or student personnel work in higher education or student affairs and they come into the profession wide-eyed and believing that they can make a true difference," Gurney said. "And slowly they find themselves to be products of a much larger system that only cares about the eligibility of student-athletes and APR numbers getting the athletes eligible at all or any cost. (Grasgreen, 2012b, para. 20)

NjCAA rules manual bylaws regarding student-athletes with learning disabilities

Academic Eligibility Exceptions:

E.1. Certified Disabled Student-Athlete Exception: A disabled NJCAA student-athlete may be eligible for reduced enrollment and accumulation requirements provided that the student-athlete notifies the member college of his/her disability prior to the beginning of the academic term AND the following regulations in this section are followed:

E.1.a. Enrollment: A disabled student-athlete may be considered full-time with enrollment in 6 to 11 credit hours per term, with the enrollment to be determined based on the institution's academic authority evaluation.

E.1.a.i. A student-athlete who registers or enrolls in 12 or more credit hours must meet the standard academic requirements prior to participation.

E.1.b. Accumulation: A disabled student athlete may substitute his/her required full-time hours as established by the academic authority evaluation for the factor of 12 in accumulation requirements which shall be multiplied by the number of modified full-time terms.

E.1.c. Second Season Participant (relief from the 24 semester/36 quarter hours)
The minimum requirement of credit hours would vary between 12-22 semester/18-33 quarter hours coupled with a 2.00 GPA for Certified Disabled Student-Athletes prior to their second season of competition.

E.1.d. Documentation Requirements: The following documents must be submitted and an approval granted by the NJCAA National Office prior to any participation by the disabled student-athlete in an NJCAA certified sport who does not meet the standard NJCAA requirements:

E.1.d.i.   A written copy of the institution's policies and curriculum guidelines applicable to all disabled students.

E.1.d.ii. A completed NJCAA Certified Learning Disabled Student-Athlete Request form.

E.1.d.iii. Written documentation from an appropriate institutional academic authority (registrar, for example) at the student-athlete's institution of participation dictating that the institution has de need the student-athlete's full-time enrollment to be less than 12 credit hours to compensate for the student-athlete's disability. Student-athlete's current class schedule.

E.1.d.iv. Student-athlete's current class schedule.

E.1.d.v. Written documentation that describes the application of the institution's policies to the student-athlete in question and documentation that indicates that institutional support and accommodation, though signi cant, is insu cient to address the academic needs of disabled student-athletes.

E.1.d.vi. A summary of support services and other accommodations provided by the applicant's institution designed to assist the disabled student-athlete, expected to include:

E.1.d.vi.a. Written and signed diagnosis of the disability, including the results of specific measures or tests, which formed the basis of the diagnosis.

E.1.d.vi.b. A copy of the student-athlete's Individual Education Plan (IEP), if applicable.

E.1.d.vi.c. Name, position and signature of the qualified individual issuing the diagnosis; this individual's professional credentials must be provided. Athletic department officials may not provide the diagnosis.

E.1.d.vi.d. Diagnosis must be current and within three (3) years of application; If specific circumstances of the case indicate that this requirement is unnecessary, an earlier diagnosis may be acceptable.

E.1.e.   Proper Submission: All required information must be submitted to the NJCAA National Office prior to any participation by the student-athlete in an NJCAA certified sport; and waiver requests must be signed by any two of the following: the Director of Athletics, the College President (Chief Executive Officer), or NJCAA Designated Representative.

E.1.f. Second Opinion: The NJCAA reserves the right to request a second opinion or diagnosis, the cost of which shall be borne by the requesting member institution.

Source: NJCAA 2016–17 rules manual.

Figure 4.3. NJCAA rules manual bylaws regarding student-athletes with learning disabilities

All of these academic rules lead to a variety of consequences for academic practitioners. Clearly, with the NCAA leading the charge down a road of increasing academic requirements and standardized measures of academic success, there are many bylaws and regulations that must be followed by student-athletes. In turn, the responsibility falls upon athletic academic counselors and other practitioners within the athletic academic services office and athletic compliance office to monitor and ensure student-athletes continue to meet the standards set by the governing body to which they adhere. But therein lies the problem. Athletic academic counseling has become a profession burdened by a system focused on eligibility at all costs rather than one where professionals can make a meaningful difference in the academic and professional lives of student-athletes. A 2012 article from *Inside Higher Ed* revealed the concerns of industry professionals, as voiced by the then-president of N4A, Joseph P. Luckey:

> That shadow of APR and eligibility rules—it's just like a cloud that's looming over us constantly. The focus is more about those things than worrying about, is this kid growing academically, is this kid growing as an individual, is this student ready for life after college? (Grasgreen, 2012b, para. 5)

Measures of academic success for student-athletes have become standardized. This is evident with the NCAA's growing oversight and penalties for student-athletes, teams, and schools that do not live up to the given standards. It is hard to gauge the feedback on the way the NAIA and NJCAA handles student-athlete academics, as most of the mainstream media tends to focus on the most elite level of college athletics found under NCAA purview. But recently, the level at which NJCAA schools are competing and the strain under which academic counselors work was pushed into public view via the Netflix series *Last Chance U* (Whiteley, 2016). The miniseries, which focused on East Mississippi Community College, focused on the football team's advisor, who struggled to keep student-athletes motivated and prepared for class despite her strict yet caring attitude. It was clear she had the best of intentions to help the student-athletes grow, however, her main charge was to help those student-athletes meet the standards that would make them eligible to transfer to an NCAA institution.

The stories presented as a result of the academic standards that exist are the same. Advisors and counselors that work with student-athletes are stuck in a gray area between the desire to help them become academically and professionally successful. This is coupled with the pressure to ensure they meet the minimum academic standards. As observed by Grasgreen (2012b), when talking to academic counselors about their balancing act between education and eligibility, she stated "it's clear that the philosophical quandary sometimes posed by the NCAA's academic standards weighs heavily on advisers' minds" (Grasgreen, 2012b, para. 7). The philosophical quandary is the culprit not only for the increasing number of academic fraud and misconduct cases brought forth by the NCAA (Grasgreen, 2012a), but also the noted burnout experienced by academic counselors who work with student-athletes (Wolverton, 2015).

Motivation

As Grasgreen (2012b) found in talking to counselors for her continued coverage of student-athlete academics for *Inside Higher Ed,* there is not one specific background of the academic counselor in athletics. While a quick glance through current job openings reveal the majority of athletic academic support programs are looking for practitioners who hold a master's degree, a uniform path does not exist in terms of what academic major the degree was obtained or experience level. The profession is filled with former student-athletes, and young professionals with master's degrees ranging from counseling to higher education to sport management, who have aspirations to help, guide, and make a difference in the lives of the young people with which they work. Unfortunately, a growing number of reports and research studies show the ever-increasing academic standards are leading to an increasing number of coaches putting pressure on athletic counselors to ensure student-athletes are eligible to play. These particular actions are occurring regardless of overall academic performance or goals. Even more trepidation surrounds the idea this pressure shifts the perceived purpose of these jobs. This forces practitioners to the point of desperation where they feel they must act in the ethical gray area in order to ensure student-athletes maintain eligibility (New, 2016; Wolverton, 2015).

The fears that practitioners advising and counseling in a way to meet or somehow "play" the rules to keep students eligible would increase as academic requirements increased has been confirmed on more than one occasion. Various studies conducted to gauge counselor and student-athlete feelings on the academic requirements for eligibility have shown this increase in such behavior (Castle, Ammon, & Myers, 2014; Kulics, 2006). When surveying both student-athletes and athletics administrators about the increased academic requirements brought forth by the NCAA in 2003, Kulics (2006) found 15% of student-athletes admitted an academic counselor or advisor had recommended to them a major change for the purpose of athletic eligibility. Sixty percent of administrators in the study indicated they advised a student-athlete to change her or his major for the purpose of remaining eligible for athletic competition. Castle et al. (2014) conducted a similar study, but looked particularly at a 2011 rule change which increased the requirement for football student-athletes to pass nine semester hours in the fall semester to be eligible for the following season. In their research, respondents revealed this rule change impacted the way practitioners worked with the student-athletes they advised. The results indicated 57.2% of the 121 respondents would at least "slightly" change the way they advised football student-athletes. Nearly 70% indicated they were "slightly" more likely to change the way they worked with at-risk football student-athletes. More than the numbers alone, the responses the researchers gathered from the open-ended questions included in their survey showed the pessimism of practitioners regarding the increased academic requirements. One respondent indicated the only change he/she felt would come from the increased credit hour rule for football student-athletes was an increase in clustering these student-athletes within just a few "easy" majors. Another respondent indicated the increase in academic requirements would undoubtedly force athletic academic practitioners to make the decision of promoting academic choice or athletic eligibility:

> I fear that this rule will unintentionally penalize student-athletes who would otherwise have a solid chance of completing a degree but must 'settle' for an alternative for fear of jeopardizing their future eligibility. (Castle et al., 2014, p. 63)

While the research by Castle et al. focuses on football and the individual rule that applies only to that sport at the NCAA Division I level, they illuminate the frustrations and compromising positions that come with being an advisor of student-athletes.

Through academic research (Castle et al., 2014; Christy et al., 2008; Kulics, 2006) as well as numerous of articles in the media (Grasgreen, 2012a, 2012b; New, 2016; Wolverton, 2015), it has become increasingly clear the negative impact on the practitioners that work with student-athletes in an academic setting. Although many who enter this profession indicate they do so to make a change, after spending time doing the job they thought was about making a meaningful impact on the academic, personal, and professional lives of student-athletes, many reflect back on a job that has become much more about athletic eligibility than student learning.

> "It's not as simple as providing tutoring, mentoring, advising to students," Luckey said. "It's gotten more about tracking the students, the numbers, the research, so that I often find there's days that I spend more time doing reports to the NCAA and other things than I actually do sitting in an office with students in front of me." (Grasgreen, 2012b, para. 28)

Burnout

> Academic advisers like Mr. Collier are an essential part of the athletic en-
> terprise, but they have largely thankless jobs. The pay is low, the hours are
> long, and the stress of keeping players eligible has led to rapid turnover in
> the profession. (Wolverton, 2015, para. 8)

The increasing pressure to keep student-athletes academically eligible
for athletic competition while these academic requirements continue to rise
has not been without consequences. Over the past 5 years, as the implications of increased stakes being placed on team APR scores, and PTD have
come to settle, burnout amongst professionals (Grasgreen, 2012a, 2012b;
Wolverton, 2015), and academic misconduct involving academic support
staff has continued to rise (New, 2016). According to the NCAA's legislative database, more than 90 cases of academic misconduct and academic
fraud have come to fruition since the 2003 reform package went into effect
(NCAA, 2017).

As some have noted, an increase in burnout has been experienced by
athletic academic counselors since the academic reform packages of 2003,
as practitioners increasingly feel the weight of their advice and decisions
regarding student-athletes in terms of what that means for their athletic eligibility (Castle et al., 2014; Christy et al., 2008; Grasgreen, 2012a, 2012b;
Kulics, 2006; Wolverton, 2015). In cases of academic fraud, regardless of
the pressure felt from coaches or potentially even direct requests from
coaches that an advisor act in a certain way, often the athletic academic
professional is held responsible.

Burnout experienced from the increasingly high stakes these professionals face as increased academic standards for athletic eligibility often fall on
their shoulders is not uncommon. Grasgreen (2012b) interviewed athletic
academic counselors at an annual N4A convention and reported that many
of them indicated it was not uncommon for them to leave the field after
just a few years. In fact, she noted it was difficult for her to find someone to
talk to that had been in the field for more than 5 or 6 years. This was aided
in part with the fact that there is often very little upward mobility in the
profession. This leaves practitioners to decide between staying in the same
position for little pay with only small pay increases, or leave the profession
after succumbing to eligibility pressures or feeling they have come to an
end in their professional development.

Everything regarding work with student-athletes in an academic setting
is not bad, nor are advisors who work specifically with the student-athlete
population are those who have to deal with burnout. Academic advising
as a profession is known for burnout, according to the National Academic
Advising Association (NACADA), which has published numerous resources

on its website for advisors who feel the stress of the profession is sometimes too much to handle (Huebner, 2011). But, with all of this research indicating ethical dilemmas surrounding academics, burnout, and questioning the validity and reliability of using APR, PTD, and other standardized measurement tools to judge academic achievement, the question then becomes, what can we do to make this better? How can we as professionals act to more accurately gauge the academic success of the student-athletes with which we work, and better promote learning and success?

SUGGESTIONS FOR IMPROVEMENT

As previously stated, many counselors feel their primary role is to monitor and regulate academic performance to ensure the compliance and eligibility of student-athletes. This can be problematic for many reasons (e.g., limited focus on academic and personal development), but one noteworthy concern is traditional measures used to monitor student-athlete academic achievement (e.g., APR, PTD) lack the sensitivity to assess (1) academic achievement of student-athletes at risk for academic failure, and (2) the effectiveness of academic support for these individuals. The following section makes the recommendation to shift emphasis from *macro* monitoring of student athletes deemed at-risk to *micro* monitoring.

Macro Monitoring

Macro (n.d.) is defined as, "being large or exceptionally prominent." In the world of collegiate athletics, academic performance measures can be traditionally classified as macro. For the purpose of this chapter, these measures (i.e., APR, GSR, and PTD) are defined as macro because they focus on the larger goal of student-athlete eligibility and degree completion. Few people would disagree about the significance of eligibility and degree completion to student-athletes' success, but for countless student-athletes who struggle academically, these measures fail to monitor the quality of the education they receive. For many counselors, the emphasis on eligibility coupled with the pressure to maintain it, easily take priority over supporting the individual academic growth of their student-athletes (particular those who struggle).

> Levar is a redshirt freshman and the starting guard for his university. Although he has seen much success on the court, he has had to overcome some serious challenges in the classroom. For as long as Levar could remember he struggled with a language-based learning disability which caused him to have great difficulty in the areas of reading, writing, and communication. Despite Levar's challenges he was probably the hardest working student that

I have ever had the pleasure of meeting. He showed up to his tutoring appointments early and left late. Unfortunately, Levar was always the primary topic of academic coaching meetings and I constantly felt the pressure of being accountable for his academic success. Instead of focusing my attention on getting Levar the support he need to close his gaps in knowledge, I found myself flooding his time with content tutoring to keep him afloat in the classroom, and monitoring his grades to ensure he was eligible or at least to prevent any surprises to the coaches. It is difficult to accept but this was the only way I felt I could demonstrate that his time was not being wasted in my care. (Power 5 Conference Academic Counselor. *Name has been changed to synonyms to protect the identity of the student-athlete.*)

Many practitioners have encountered a Levar and found themselves frustrated at the reality his hard work and academic growth in addition to their personal effort would virtually go unnoticed as a result of how student-athletes and their support services are evaluated.

Micro Monitoring

Micro monitoring takes a different approach and focuses on the measurement of small increments of student academic growth. These include but are not limited to grammar, spelling, reading fluency, comprehension, and so forth, and represent the skills that lead to independent learning.

The premise behind micro monitoring is the ability to track and document the small changes in academic behavior. For example, research illustrates successful adolescent readers, depending on the difficulty of the text, read 120–170 correct words per minute (Tindal, Hasbrouk, & Jones, 2005). If Levar entered into his university reading well below grade level (e.g., 40 correct words per minute), it would be extremely difficult for him to read through 12 credit hours of college-level reading assignments regardless of his effort. In this situation macro monitoring might cause staff to question his determination due to his limited productivity, but micro monitoring would enable academic support personnel with a framework to monitor Levar's fluency growth overtime.

Monitoring small increments of academic growth can be intrinsically motivating for student-athletes who struggle academically (particularly those with a history of academic failure), and provide meaningful data to present to student-athlete stakeholders (e.g., coaches). This is critical to combat perceptions that eligibility monitoring is the primary role of student-athlete academic support offices. These measurements also enable staff to make data-based decisions to individualize and provide targeted supports to student-athletes who are academically at-risk. Data can also be easily collected using widely recognized assessments such as curriculum-based measures (CBM), which are designed to track the growth of basic academic areas. It should be noted these duties must be executed and led by a qualified intervention or learning specialist.

CONCLUSION

Many academic counselors, regardless of their governing body, face real challenges to support student-athletes' academic success while navigating the policies and regulations that govern their work. This ongoing pressure has led many practitioners to regard their work with student-athletes as eligibility centered with minor focus on the quality of student learning. As documented in the chapter, the ethos of student-athlete academic services is centered on retention and eligibility with the ultimate goal of graduating student-athletes. This widely accepted philosophy operates on the assumption that the necessary content mastery and learning required for independent and productive citizenship post athletics are the by-product of eligibility and retention focused ideologies. In other words, students who graduate by nature of graduation have gained essential skills for independence. This assumption has placed many student-athletes deemed academically at risk in jeopardy. Rather than advocating for individualized services that improve content/skill mastery, academic support staff, university advisors, and student-athletes often collaborate to engineer individualized course schedules that minimize the potential barriers to graduation.

Although many practitioners who work directly with academically at-risk student-athletes experience frustration (even burnout) with this practice, ultimately their actions are reinforced by rules and regulations such as PTD and FTE. It is unlikely that governing bodies (e.g., NCAA) will adapt their philosophies in the foreseeable future, but academic support staff can immediately implement change by simply adjusting how they monitor student learning. The current authors advocate student support service offices emphasize micro monitoring techniques in addition to the traditional measures that currently govern student-athlete support.

REFERENCES

Brown, R. W. (1996). The revenues associated with relaxing admission standards at division IA colleges. *Applied Economics, 28*(7), 807–814.

Castle, J., Ammon, R., & Myers, L. (2014). The 9 credit rule: A look at its impact on academic advising for intercollegiate football athletes. *Journal of Physical Education and Sport Management, 5*(5), 59–65.

Christy, K., Seifried, C., & Pastore, D. L. (2008). Intercollegiate athletics: A preliminary study examining the opinions on the impact of the academic performance rate (APR). *Journal of Issues in Intercollegiate Athletics, (1)*1–10.

Grasgreen, A. (2012a, April 20). More credits, more clusters. *Inside Higher Ed.* Retrieved from https://www.insidehighered.com/news/2012/04/20/football-advisers-predict-negative-athlete-outcomes-under-9-credit-rule

Grasgreen, A. (2012b, May 9). Tough choices for athletes' advisers. *Inside Higher Ed.* Retrieved from https://www.insidehighered.com/news/2012/05/09/ncaa-academic-rules-frustrate-advisers-athletes

Gurney, G. S. (2011). Stop lowering the bar for college athletes. *Chronicle of Higher Education, 57*(32), A30.

Hamilton, K. (2005). Putting the 'student' back into the student-athlete: In an effort to improve retention and graduation rates, the NCAA rolls out new rules and regulations. *Black Issues in Higher Education, 22,* 1–7.

Hosick, M. (2011). New rule should boost APR in football. *The NCAA News.* Retrieved from http://www.ncaa.org/wps/wcm/connect/public/NCAA/Resources/Latest+News/2011/May/New+rule+should+boost+APRs+in+football

Huebner, C. (2011). Caring for the caregivers: Strategies to overcome the effects of job burnout. Retrieved from NACADA Clearinghouse of Academic Advising Resources website http://www.nacada.ksu.edu/Resources/Clearinghouse/View-

Kulics, J. (2006). An analysis of the academic behaviors and beliefs of Division I student-athletes and academic administrators: The impact of the increased percentage toward degree requirements (Doctoral dissertation). Retrieved from https://www.kent.edu/sites/default/files/file/KulicsJennifer.pdf

Macro. (n.d.). *Merriam-Webster Online.* In Merriam-Webster. Retrieved from https://www.merriam-webster.com/dictionary/macro

NAIA (2018). NAIA Eligibility. Retrieved from https://www.playnaia.org/page/eligibility.php

National Association of Intercollegiate Athletics (NAIA). *2016–2017 Official Policy Handbook.* (2016). Retrieved from http://www.naia.org/ViewArticle.dbml?ATCLID=205327260

National Association of Academic Advisors for Athletics. (September 2004). Practices and concepts for the success of NCAA academic reform. National Association of Academic Advisors for Athletes. Raleigh, NC: McDonnell, S.

National Collegiate Athletic Association (NCAA). (2014a). *2014 Division I graduation success rate aggregate data.* Retrieved from http://www.ncaa.org/sites/default/files/2014-d1-grad-rate-aggregate.pdf

National Collegiate Athletic Association (NCAA). (2014b). *Academic Progress Rate (APR).* Retrieved from http://www.ncaa.org/about/resources/research/academic-progress-rate-aprNational Collegiate Athletic Association (NCAA). *APR Public Recognition Awards.* (2016). Retrieved from http://web1.ncaa.org/maps/aprRecognitionAwards.jsp

National Collegiate Athletic Association (NCAA). 2016–17 NCAA Division I Rules Manual. (2016). Retrieved from http://www.ncaapublications.com/p-4435-2016-2017-ncaa-division-i-manual-august-version-available-august-2016.aspx

National Collegiate Athletic Association (NCAA). *Legislative Services Database (LSDBi)*. (2017). Accessed February 20, 2017, https://web3.ncaa.org/lsdbi/

National Junior College Athletic Association (NJCAA). *2016-17 Eligibility Rules Pamphlet*. (2016). Retrieved from http://www.njcaa.org/eligibility/eligibility_rules

New, J. (2016, July 8). An 'Epidemic' of academic fraud. *Inside Higher Ed*. Retrieved from https://www.insidehighered.com/news/2016/07/08/more-dozen-athletic-programs-have-committed-academic-fraud-last-decade-more-likely

Purdy, D.A., Eitzen, D. S., & Hufnagel, R. (1982). Are athletes also students? The educational attainment of college athletes. *Social Problems, 29*(4), 439–448.

Singleton, A. (2013). A history of the National Collegiate Athletic Association's academic reform movement and analysis of the Academic Progress Rate in Division I-A Institutions (Doctoral dissertation). Retrieved from http://mars.gmu.edu/jspui/bitstream/handle/1920/8760/Singleton_gmu_0883E_10469.pdf?sequence=1&isAllowed=y

Tindal, G., Hasbrouck, J., & Jones, C. (2005). Oral reading fluency: 90 years of measurement. *Behavioral Research and Teaching Technical Report, 33*.

Whiteley, G. (2016). Last change U on Netflix Original. USA. Retrieved June 13, 2017, from https://www.netflix.com/title/80091742Wolverton, B. (2015, October 11). Missed classes, a changed grade, and one disillusioned adviser. *The Chronicle of Higher Education*. Retrieved from http://www.chronicle.com/article/Missed-Classes-a-Changed/233717

Winters, C. A., & Gurney, G. S. (2012). Academic preparation of specially-admitted student-athletes: A question of basic skills. *College and University, 88*(2), 2.

CHAPTER 5

MOTIVATING STUDENT-ATHLETES FOR ACADEMIC SUCCESS

Joy Gaston Gayles, Robert Lang, and Ezinne Ofoegbu
North Carolina State University

ABSTRACT

This chapter focuses on some of the challenges that student-athletes face from the demands of balancing academic and athletic tasks, and how these experiences shape motivation for academic success. Using achievement motivation theory as a frame of reference, we conclude the chapter with an overview of the literature on a student-athlete motivation and offer strategies for improving motivation through assessment and building academic resilience.

The Collegiate Athlete At Risk:
Strategies for Academic Support and Success, pp. 77–91
Copyright © 2019 by Information Age Publishing

Introduction

The research literature documents that student-athletes face challenges during the college years in ways different from their nonathlete peers (Gayles & Hu, 2009; Paule & Gibson, 2011; Watt & Moore, 2001; Wolverton, 2008). All college students are expected to navigate a range of cognitive and affective developmental tasks during their college years (Mayhew, Bowman, Rockenbach, Seifert, & Wolniak, 2016). Participation in competitive college sports can complicate student development making it difficult to balance the academic, social, and athletic tasks during college (Adler & Adler, 1991; Comeaux & Harrison, 2011; Jolly, 2008). Student-athletes are required to take a full schedule of classes each semester, practice 20 hours per week, complete homework assignments and group projects, attend study hall and travel during competition season for away games. Such a demanding schedule leaves little time and energy for socialization experiences with peers, which are also vital to learning and personal development in college (Comeaux & Harrison, 2011; Gayles & Hu, 2009). Maintaining motivation to be successful in academics and athletics can be challenging without support and guidance from the college environment. This chapter focuses on strategies to improve student-athletes' motivation towards academic success by first discussing some of the challenges they face related to academic standards and degree attainment. We then turn our attention to the growing body of literature on motivation and student-athletes. The chapter concludes with a discussion of potential strategies to motivate student-athletes for academic success.

Academic Standards for Student-Athletes

Over the last decade, the National Collegiate Athletic Association's (NCAA) academic eligibility requirements have grown drastically, now including benchmarks for credit hours, grade point average (GPA), and progress toward degree completion. All student-athletes are required to pass six quarter/semester credits per regular academic term, except for football student-athletes, who must pass nine quarter/semester credits in the fall term (NCAA, 2017). However, during the academic year (not including summer terms), student-athletes are required to pass at least 18 semester or 27 quarter credits. This rule encourages all student-athletes to pass at least nine credits per regular academic term, keeping their course load and rigor consistent each term. Before the beginning of each semester, student-athletes are required to meet a set of academic benchmarks that determine whether or not they are eligible to play their sport in the subsequent semester. Prior to their second year, student-athletes are required to complete at least 24 semester or 36 quarter hours and achieve at least a 1.8 GPA. By their third year, student-athletes are required to have 40% of their degree hours completed and achieve at least a 1.9 GPA. Courses outside of their prerequisite and major courses, and any university required courses (e.g., general education), do not count toward the 40% rule. Prior to their fourth year, student-athletes are required to have 60% of their major coursework completed, as well as maintain a 2.0 GPA until graduation. Prior to their fifth year, student-athletes are required to have 80% of the degree program completed.

Although the aforementioned benchmarks are meant to hold student-athletes accountable, students in the general population are not held to any standards for matriculation to degree completion and have the freedom to select a major when they choose, drop a course, earn below a "C" in a course, or retake a course without penalty. However, meeting these benchmarks helps ensure their bachelor's degree completion within 5 years. In some ways, student-athletes can be motivated by fear of failure to meet these standards, which is not ideal for facilitating academic success. Student-athletes who find it challenging to balance academics and athletics and spend more time and effort on academic tasks may need more academic support and supplemental instruction to bolster success.

Academic Issues and Degree Attainment for Student-Athletes

For some student-athletes, academic challenges begin before they enroll in college. Winters and Gurney (2012) found the NCAA's sliding scale for initial academic eligibility and special admissions practices for student-athletes allow student-athletes with higher high school GPAs, but lower standardized test scores to enter college under special admission. Although high school grades and standardized test scores are not the best predictors of future performance, they continue to be the most commonly used measures for making admissions decisions (Gayles & Baker, 2015). Because of inequities in schools across the country some students have difficulty adjusting to the academic rigor once they enter college. Student-athletes who enter college with high academic performance records from under-resourced high schools may struggle with adjusting to the academic rigor during the first year of college (Gayles & Baker, 2015; McArdle, Paskus, & Boker, 2013). Adding the challenge of balancing roles as a student and an athlete to adjusting to the academic rigor of the institution can be overwhelming and discouraging if not managed well (Gayles & Baker, 2015; Howard-Hamilton & Sina, 2001; Potuto & O'Hanlon, 2007; Watt & Moore, 2001). Paule and Gibson (2011) explained participation in athletics made it challenging to develop and maintain useful study skills and complete assignments in a timely fashion. While most instructions and athletic programs provide supplemental instruction and academic support such as tutors, exam reviews, and study groups, administrators find their challenge lies in convincing the student-athletes to go beyond the goal of maintaining academic eligibility to developing an internal drive for academic success (Comeaux, 2015; Gaston-Gayles, 2004).

There are many ways to measure student-athletes' academic success. In 2002, the NCAA implemented the Graduation Success Rate (GSR), which measures the extent to which student-athletes are earning college degrees (Brown, 2014). The GSR excludes from an institution's calculation student-athletes who transferred to another institution while academically eligible and includes student-athletes who transferred to the institution and completed their degrees, whereas the Federal Graduation Rate (FGR) counts both of these student-athletes as nongraduates for their prior institutions (NCAA, 2016). Similar to the FGR, the GSR tracks 6-year cohorts of student-athletes. There has been much debate about which rate best captures and reflects how well student-athletes are matriculating through college at NCAA institutions. In 2016, the GSR of student-athletes at Division 1 institutions was 86%, in comparison to the FGR of student-athletes and non-athletes at Division 1 institutions, both at 66% (NCAA, 2016). Student-athletes respond differently to the challenges associated with balancing academics and athletics and maintaining eligibility requirements. Some student-athletes strike a balance and perform well in academics and athletics while other student-athletes do not. The following section focuses on the role motivation plays in the academic success of student-athletes.

Achievement Motivation

Motivation is defined as the intensity and direction of behavior (Silva & Weinberg, 1984). Intensity refers to how much effort an individual applies toward a task, and direction involves whether or not an individual decides to complete a task. Student-athletes have dual identities informed by their participation in college sports and their status as a college student. The extent to which student-athletes are motivated to apply effort, and complete tasks in both athletics and academics is an essential area of interest. Achievement motivation theories explain how people choose and persist on tasks, as well as the amount of enthusiasm about and overall performance on a task (Wigfield & Eccles, 2000). Several motivation theories and perspectives that fall under the achievement motivation umbrella.

Expectancy-value theory suggests there are two major determinants for motivation to achieve a task (Spence & Helmreich, 1983). The first determinant involves the probability the task will be completed successfully, and the second determinant involves the value associated with completing the task. For example, the motivation to participate in college sports for a student-athlete is informed by the extent to which students perceive they can be successful as a college athlete, as well as the value they associate with competing as a college athlete. Expectancy, or the probability of completing a task successfully, is influenced by an individual's self-concept, or how good they perceive themselves to be in a task domain, as well as the level of difficulty associated with completing the task (Eccles, 1983). The value aspect of this theory involves the extent to which the task fulfills a need or aids in goal attainment. The attractiveness or success or failure on a task also plays into how much or little the task is valued. Both expectancies, or judgments about the probability of completing a task, and the value associated with the task inform anticipated success or failure on a task, and individuals use this information in their decision to approach or avoid a task (Atkinson, 1957).

Self-efficacy theory (Bandura, 1986) and self-worth theory (Covington, 1992) also play a role in achievement motivation and expectancy-value theory. Bandura (1986) defined self-efficacy as a person's judgment about his or her ability to complete a task successfully. As a result, individuals will approach tasks they believe they can complete successfully and avoid tasks they do not think they can complete successfully. Self-worth theory (Covington, 1992) suggests individuals have certain beliefs about their abilities, and their sense of positive self-worth is preserved by maintaining positive beliefs about their abilities. Covington (1992) also suggested individuals have a fundamental need to protect their value or sense of worth. Further, how people think about their abilities is critical to the self-protection process because an individual's sense of self-worth connects to competence. As a result, individuals who are talented, skilled, or have high ability also have a strong sense of worthiness.

Academic resilience is a psychological construct related to motivation, particularly regarding the capacity of individuals to bounce back when they experience academic failure. Academic resilience refers to an individual's "capacity to overcome acute and/or chronic adversity that is seen as a major threat to a student's educational development" (Martin, 2013, p. 48). For student-athletes, it involves how well they can bounce back when they experience a setback. For example, if a student-athlete performs poorly on a math test, to what extent can he or she regroup to earn a passing math grade? Academic resilience can be useful in explaining why some students achieve and excel in the face of challenges and setbacks and why other students do not.

Academic resilience does not determine emotional stability; instead, individuals who are academically resilient have characteristics or traits that propel them to keep trying after experiencing a setback. Individuals who have a high degree of academic resilience are likely to be persistent, enthusiastic, and have clear goals related to tasks. Both internal and external factors inform academic resilience. Internal factors include goal setting, motivation, internal locus of control, and high self-efficacy (Hartley, 2011; McMillan & Reed, 1994; Morales, 2008; Waxman, Gray, & Padron, 2002). External factors connected to academic resilience include high expectations and encouragement from family, peers, and mentors (Garmezy, 1991).

Is it possible to teach student-athletes how to increase their academic resilience? In other words, how can advisors, campus administrators, and counselors facilitate or increase a student's capacity or ability to bounce back when they experience a setback, particularly in the academic domain? One approach to building a student's resilience muscle is through teaching growth mindset principles. Carol Dweck (2008) suggests shifting the way individuals think about intelligence and the role of effort and hard work in the process of achieving a goal can have a profound influence on learning and goal attainment. Through her research studying how children respond in the face of increasingly difficult tasks, she identified two types of mindsets: fixed and growth (Dweck, 2006). The basic assumption undergirding a fixed mindset is the belief aptitude and intelligence are not changeable. However, the underlying assumption for growth mindset is intelligence can be improved through hard work and effort. No two people are the same; however, the major premise behind growth mindset is that people's initial talents, interests, and capabilities can change in positive ways through persistence, attitude, and time on task.

Student-Athletes and Motivation

When examining the role of motivation for student-athletes, it is important to acknowledge that motivation as a student may differ from their drive as an athlete (Gaston-Gayles, 2004, 2005). Some student-athletes enter college with aspirations to compete at an elite or professional level in their sport. Beamon and Bell (2004) compared the professional career aspirations of African American and Caucasian student-athletes, and the effects these aspirations have on their attitudes toward academics. This study found African American children from low-income backgrounds grow up with the perception of sport participation as a means to economic and social mobility. As a result, some African American children carry this belief into their college experience and are driven by athletic success to the detriment of academic success (Johnson, Wessel, & Pierce, 2013). Having high athletic motivation coupled with low of academic motivation is even more significant for athletes playing revenue-generating sports, which happen to be dispro-portionately populated with African Americans students (Gaston-Gayles, 2004; Paule & Gilson, 2011). In comparison, White children from affluent communities grow up having the capital, more often than not, to be academically prepared for university-level coursework, making their dependence on college athletics for economic mobility less likely (Beamon & Bell, 2004). Precollege aptitude and performance are common indicators of how a student-athlete will perform in college, but noncognitive factors are important as well. In a foundational study the importance of noncogntive factors, Tracey and Sedlacek (1982) examined the effectiveness of the Noncognitive Questionnaire (NCQ) in predicting the first-year performance of college students. The NCQ is a questionnaire that assesses eight noncognitive variables believed to predict college performance. Tracey and Sedlacek found noncognitive variables, in addition to SAT scores, increased the prediction of GPA and the likelihood of retention. Sedlacek and Adams-Gaston (1992) also found a relationship between the NCQ and college GPA, but no relationship between the SAT scores and college GPA. The latter claim supports another study where the authors found significant relationships between positive self-concept and the creation of long-term goals and positive academic performance and persistence (Ting, 2009). Since the SAT is considered "the gold standard" to measure how prepared a high school student is for college, a higher score on this test may result in a greater sense of academic self-worth (Wiley, Shavelson, & Kurpius, 2014). Once student-athletes arrive on their college campus, how do they develop and sustain academic motivation? Woodruff and Schallert (2008) explored the motivation sense of self, or the relationship between motivation and self, within the realms of athletics and academics. This study identified five types of student-athletes: (1) "stay to play," (2) "what am I doing here?", (3) "the best of the both," (4) "sports aren't everything," and (5) "the student." Those student-athletes who fell into groups 1, 3, and 5 had a clear understanding of their goals, whether their priority was being successful athletically, succeeding academically, or balancing both. Those student-athletes who aligned with groups 2 and 4 experienced more challenges in identifying their goals but were more interested in one identity than the other. Similarly, Simons, Van Rheenen, and Covington (1999) suggest student-athletes are either motivated to succeed or to avoid failure. Their study applied the self-worth theory's four motivational types—success-oriented, overstrivers, failure-avoiders, and failure acceptors—to student-athletes at a Division 1 institution. Student-athletes who belonged to the success-oriented type possessed better reading and study skills and had a greater sense of academic self-worth. While overstrivers also possessed the same study habits as those who are self-motivated, they more often faced challenges with reading and studying, which resulted in a lower sense of academic self-worth. The "dumb jock" stereotype threat, or the possibility other students and faculty will perceive student-athletes as academically inferior because of their athletic identity, could instill feelings of doubt in their academic abilities (Dee, 2014). Not only could this align with the overstriver behavior, it can also align with the failure-orientated motivation types. Failure-avoiders are driven by the fear of failing, which comes at the expense of striving for academic success, and possess a lower sense of academic self-worth, while failure accepters are overly concerned with success or failure (Simons et al., 1999). For failure-avoiders and accepters, their athletic motivations outweigh their academic motivations, which explains their consideration of possibly failing for fear of being deemed academically ineligible. Furthermore, student-athletes in revenue-generating sports had larger amounts of failure-acceptors and avoiders, leading Simons et al. (1999) to conclude the added external pressure these sports apply to their students has a negative effect on their academic self-worth.

Overminer and Lawry's theory of incentive motivation states incentives can improve performance by mediating between a stimulus and the desired response (Tuckman, 1996). For example, Readdy, Raabe, and Harding (2014) assessed the effectiveness of an off-season rewards program for football student-athletes at a Division 1 institution. In this scenario, the stimuli were tangible rewards and public recognition, while the desired response was doing well academically, which was monitored on a weekly basis. A majority of the participants felt the program did little to motivate them academically; however, a few participants were motivated by the competition the program created among their teammates and the public recognition they received for doing well. A similar study assessed the effectiveness of the autonomy-supportive coaching style, which encourages student-athletes to set their own goals and create their own sources of motivation while the coach provides support and guidance. The more the coaches supported the student-athletes' goals, the more the student-athlete experienced fulfillment of three key needs: competence, autonomy, and relatedness (Amorose & Anderson-Butcher, 2007). This autonomous-supportive coaching style could also be useful within academics by way of their advisors, mentors, and tutors, for example. Furthermore, Thompson and Gregory (2012) suggest professionals who work with student-athletes should be intentional about building rapport and establishing trust between themselves and their athletes. It is especially important for these professionals to recognize their academic and personal priorities are just as important as their athletic priorities (Broughton & Neyer, 2001). In addition, research has shown student-athletes make decisions based on how their coaches will react (Comeaux & Harrison, 2011; Simons, Rheenen, & Covington, 1999). For example, if a student-athlete chose to attend an academic-related event, as opposed to an optional workout, they deal with the fear this action will result in them not starting or playing at all in their next game. Coaches should encourage such behavior. Prioritizing responsibilities and making tough choices among competing demands are essential life skills.

METHODS TO IMPROVE MOTIVATION FOR STUDENT-ATHLETES

Assessing Student-Athletes' Motivation

One strategy for improving student athlete's academic performance is to assess how motivated they are toward academic-related tasks. The Student-Athletes' Motivation toward Sports and Academics Questionnaire (SAMSAQ) (Gaston-Gayles, 2005) was designed to measure the extent to which college athletes are motivated to achieve in academics and athletics at the college level. The SAMSAQ consists of three subscales that measure three different types of motivation: (1) academic motivation, (2) student athletic motivation, and (3) career athletic motivation. Academic motivation consists of 16 items that measure the extent to which student-athletes are motivated to achieve academic-related tasks. The student athletic motivation subscale consists of eight items that measure how motivated student-athletes are to excel in their sport, without the desire to pursue their sport at an elite level. The career athletic motivation subscale consists of five items that are distinctly different from the student athletic motivation subscale because it captures motivation to pursue or play sports at an elite or professional level.

Gaston-Gayles (2004) used the SAMSAQ to examine the relationship between academic and athletic motivation and academic performance for student-athletes at a Division I institution. A major finding from this study was of the three subscales measured, academic motivation had the strongest relationship to academic performance. This finding suggests regardless of whether a student athlete is motivated to achieve in her or his sport or values playing at an elite level, what matters most is the extent to which he or she is motivated to achieve academically. This finding has been supported in other studies that have used the SAMSAQ to examine its relationship to academic performance, and the strong relationship between academic motivation and academic performance holds even in international contexts (Fortes, Rodrigues, & Tchantchane, 2010). Administrators in academic support can use the SAMSAQ as a diagnostic tool to assess the student-athletes' motivation. For student-athletes who score lower on the academic motivation subscale, an action plan can be created to help them increase their academic motivation using the tenets of expectancy-value theory and other forms of psychological perspectives such as academic resilience and growth mindset to shift how students think about failure, intelligence, and effort.

Building Academic Resilience

As described earlier in this chapter, a student athlete's motivation towards academic success is determined to a large extent by his or her perceived sense of competency and ability to develop this competency, particularly in the face of difficulty or hardship. College student-athletes regularly confront instances of academic adversity unique to their college experience, including managing demanding practice schedules (sometimes 20 hours per week or more), enduring the pain and anguish over injuries, and missing classes due to competition (Watt & Moore, 2001; Wolverton, 2008). The stress accrued from balancing academic and athletic tasks affects noncognitive psychological factors that can impede student success, particularly for Division I student-athletes. Data from a national survey on the student-athlete experience show student-athletes have less time for socialization and relaxation and are getting less sleep in 2015 than they were 5 years prior (NCAA, 2016). Further, student-athletes experience anxiety and depression as well as feelings of being intractably overwhelmed at higher rates in 2015 than 5 years prior (NCAA, 2016). Studies have also shown NCAA D-I athletes are especially prone to threats to their quality of life (QOL) (Wrisberg, 1996; Wrisberg, Johnson, & Brooks, 2000), which include the types of factors described above. Quality of life in an academic context by refers to satisfaction with the academic and social aspects of college life, including with such contributors as faculty, classroom environment, workload, on-campus housing, collegiate athletics, and others (Sirgy, Crzeskowiak, and Rahtz, 2007). This definition also considers the health aspects that comprise a student's overall well-being, consistent with most other—more traditional—conceptualizations of QOL (Costanza et al., 2008). The American Institutes for Research (1988) compared student-athletes to non-student-athletes also engaged in extracurricular activities (e.g., band) regarding QOL and found lower QOL measures for student-athletes.

Resiliency in student-athletes is related to mental toughness, or the degree to which a student-athlete remains determined, focused, confident, and in control under pressure (Connaughton, Hanton, & Jones, 2007); mental toughness is also positively associated with QOL in student-athletes (Knust, LaGuerre, Wrisberg, King, & Berggrun, 2014). To this end, Gayles and Lang (2017) designed a teachable model for helping college students build academic resilience and growth mindset. This model, called SASsy, considers social connectedness, positive attitude, and silliness (or humor) as major sources of resilience for students, adapted from a similar model by Cornell psychologist Greg Eells (TEDx, 2015). These three factors are especially important in helping athletes to develop motivation both on and off the field. For example, Monda, Etzel, Shannon, and Wooding (2015) found those student-athletes capable of handling dual roles as student and athlete and who stay motivated for both have a stronger sense of self-efficacy and a greater familial support system than their less academically successful counterparts. Similarly, Sedlacek and Adams-Gaston (1992) determined the best noncognitive predictors of first-semester grades for student-athletes were self-confidence and social support, which, as shown above, were better predictors of academic success than SAT scores.

Both of these success factors are directly related to the positive attitude and social connectedness components of the SASsy model. Student-athletes, in particular, understand the value of teamwork in winning sports competitions, and this support from their teammates, their coaches, and the greater university community, as well as from their friends and family, is integral to staying motivated and resilient in the classroom as well as on the court or on the field. Resilience is further cultivated by way of having a positive self-concept (Ting, 2009), meaning the student regards failure and academic setbacks as opportunities to learn and as chances to prove oneself rather than signs of weakness or hopelessness. Finally, because athletes have such demanding schedules, they have less time for opportunities to socialize compared to nonathletes (Watson & Kissinger, 2007), and so it is particularly important for athletes to engage with each other socially when they can, and humor plays a vital role in these socialization processes. As previously stated, athletes often must deal with injuries and with losing games, and one way to deal with these difficult circumstances is through humor. Humor has been shown to reduce symptoms of stress, build bonding relationships, and aid in the development of self-efficacy (Vereen, Butler, Williams, Darg, & Downing, 2006). As student-athletes brush themselves off with silliness during athletic competition, so too can they support each other with humor and positive attitudes in the classroom.

In conclusion, this chapter discussed some of the challenges student-athletes encounter that can influence motivation toward academic success as they attempt to balance life as a student-athlete. It is important that student-athletes learn not to be motivated by fear of failure or simply comply with rules and regulations for eligibility. Instead, it would be ideal for student-athletes to cultivate an internal drive and a positive mindset for academic success. Understanding what drives behavior and how self-perceptions and attitudes shape thinking and subsequent behavior are important sources of information that can be used to enhance academic success. Assessing student-athletes motivation using the SAMSAQ is a significant first step to understanding student-athletes' motivation. For example, an advising plan can be developed using the scale to help student-athletes increase their academic motivation if they score low on the academic subscale. Students athletes can learn how to be more academically resilient when they experience academic setbacks. Many of the same skills student-athletes use to bounce back from a loss in their sport can be applied to bounce back when they experience an academic setback. These resilience skills are transferable and can be taught to help student-athletes build their academic resilience muscle and motivate them toward academic success.

REFERENCES

Adler, P. A., & Adler, P. (1991). *Backboards & blackboards: College athletics and role engulfment.* New York, NY: Columbia University Press.

American Institutes for Research. (1988a). *Report No. 1: Summary results from the 1987-88 national study of intercollegiate athletes.* Palo Alto, CA: Center for the Study of Athletics.

Amorose, A. J., & Anderson-Butcher, D. (2015). Exploring the independent and interactive effects of autonomy-supportive and controlling coaching behaviors on adolescent athletes' motivation for sport. *Sport, Exercise, and Performance Psychology, 4*(3), 206–218.

Atkinson, J. W. (1957). Motivational determinants of risk-taking behavior. *Psychological Review, 64*(6), 359–372.

Bandura, A. (1986). *Social foundations of thought and action: A social cognitive theory.* Englewood Cliffs, NJ: Prentice-Hall.

Beamon, K., & Bell, P. A. (2006). Academics versus athletics: An examination of the effects of background and socialization on African American male student-athletes. *The Social Science Journal, 43*(3), 393–403.

Broughton, E., & Neyer, M. (2001). Advising and counseling student-athletes. *New Directions for Student Services, 2001*(93), 47–53.

Brown, G. (2014, October 28). NCAA graduation rates: A quarter-century of tracking academic success. *NCAA.* Retrieved from http://www.ncaa.org/about/resources/research/ncaa-graduation-rates-quarter-century-tracking-academic-success

Comeaux, E. (2015). Innovative research into practice in support centers for college athletes: Implications for the academic progress rate initiative. *Journal of College Student Development, 56*(3), 274–279.

Comeaux, E., & Harrison, K. C. (2011). A conceptual model of academic success for student-athletes. *Educational Researcher, 40*(5), 235–245.

Connaughton, D., Hanton, S., & Jones, G. (2007). A framework of mental toughness in the world's best performers. *The Sport Psychologist, 21,* 243–264.

Costanza. R., Fisher, B., Ali, S., Beer, C., Bond, L., Boumans, R., & Snapp, R. (2008). An integrative approach to quality of life measurement, research, and policy. *SAPIENS, 1*(1).

Dee, T. S. (2014). Stereotype threat and the student-athlete. *Economic Inquiry, 52*(1), 173–182.

Dweck, C. S. (2008). *Mindset: The new psychology of success.* Random House Digital.

Eccles, J. (1983). Expectancies, values, and academic behaviors. In J. T. Spence (Ed), *Achievement and achievement motives: Psychological and sociological approaches* (pp. 75–146). San Francisco, CA: W. H. Freeman and Company.

Fortes, P., Rodrigues, G., & Tchantchane, A. (2010). Investigation of academic and athletic motivation on academic performance among university students'. *International Journal of Trade, Economics and Finance, 1*(4), 367–372.

Garmezy, N. (1991). Resiliency and vulnerability to adverse developmental outcomes associated with poverty. *American Behavioral Scientist, 34*(4), 416–430.

Gaston-Gayles, J. G. (2004). Examining academic and athletic motivation among student-athletes at a division I university. *Journal of College Student Development, 45*(1), 75–83.

Gaston-Gayles, J. L. (2005). The factor structure and reliability of the student athletes' motivation toward sports and academics questionnaire (SAMSAQ). *Journal of College Student Development, 46*(3), 317–327.

Gayles, J. G., & Baker, A. R. (2015). Opportunities and challenges for first-year student-athletes transitioning from high school to college. *New Directions for Student Leadership, 2015*(147), 43–51.

Gayles, J. G., & Hu, S. (2009). The influence of student engagement and sport participation on college outcomes among division I student-athletes. *The Journal of Higher Education, 80*(3), 315–333.

Gayles, J. G., & Lang, R. (2017, March 29). Getting SASsy: *Building academic resilience for marginalized students.* Symposium conducted at the ACPA-College Student Educators International 2017 Annual Convention, Columbus, OH.

Hartley, M. T. (2011). Examining the relationships between resilience, mental health, and academic persistence in undergraduate college students. *Journal of American College Health, 59*(7), 596–604.

Howard-Hamilton, M. F., & Sina, J. A. (2001). How college affects student-athletes. *New Directions for Student Services, 2001*(93), 35–45.

Johnson, J. E., Wessel, R. D., & Pierce, D. A. (2013). Exploring the influence of select demographic, academic, and athletic variables on the retention of student-athletes. *Journal of College Student Retention, 15*(2), 135–155.

Jolly, J. C. (2008). Raising the question# 9 is the student-athlete population unique? And why should we care? *Communication Education, 57*(1), 145–151.

Knust, S., LaGuerre, K., Wrisberg, C., King, C., & Berggrun, N. (2014). Preliminary evidence for a relationship between mental toughness and quality of life for NCAA division-I student-athletes. *Athletic Insight, 6*(2), 173.

Mayhew, M. J., Bowman, N. A., Rockenbach, A. N., Seifert, T. A., & Wolniak, G. C. (2016). *How college affects students: 21st century evidence that higher education works* (Vol. 3). San Francisco, CA: John Wiley & Sons.

McArdle, J. J., Paskus, T. S., & Boker, S. M. (2013). A multilevel multivariate analysis of academic performances in college based on NCAA student-athletes. *Multivariate Behavioral Research, 48*(1), 57–95.

McMillan, J. H., & Reed, D. F. (1994). At-risk students and resiliency: Factors contributing to academic success. *Clearing House, 67*, 137–140.

Monda, S. J., Etzel, E. F., Shannon, V. R., & Wooding, C. B. (2015). Understanding the academic experiences of freshman football athletes: Insight for sport psychology professionals. *Athletic Insight*, 7(2), 115–128.

Morales, E. E. (2008). The resilient mind: The psychology of academic resilience. *The Education Forum*, 72, 152–167.

National Collegiate Athletic Association. (2016). Trends in graduation success rates and federal graduation rates at NCAA division I institutions. Retrieved from https://www.ncaa.org/sites/default/files/2016RES_GSRandFedTrends-Final_sc_20161114.pdf

National Collegiate Athletic Association. (2017). Division I progress-toward-degree requirements. Retrieved from http://www.ncaa.org/about/division-i-progress-toward-degree-requirements

National Collegiate Athletic Association. (2016). NCAA GOALS study of the student-athlete experience: Initial summary of findings. Retrieved from http://www.ncaa.org/sites/default/files/GOALS_2015_summary_jan2016_final_20160627.pdf

Paule, A. L., & Gilson, T. A. (2011). Does athletic participation benefit or hinder academic performance? Non-revenue sport athlete experiences. *Journal of Contemporary Athletics*, 5(3), 203–217.

Potuto, J. R., & O'Hanlon, J. (2007). National study of student-athletes regarding their experiences as college students. *College Student Journal*, 41(4), 947.

Readdy, T., Raabe, J., & Harding, J. S. (2014). Student-athletes' perceptions of an extrinsic reward program: A mixed-methods exploration of self-determination theory in the context of college football. *Journal of Applied Sport Psychology*, 26(2), 157–171.

Sedlacek, W. E., & Adams-Gaston, J. (1992). Predicting the Academic Success of Student-Athletes Using SAT and Noncognitive Variables. *Journal of Counseling & Development*, 70(6), 724–727.

Silva, J. M., III, & Weinberg, R. S. (Eds.). (1984). *Psychological foundations of sport*. Champaign, IL: Human Kinetics.

Simons, H. D., Rheenen, D. V., & Covington, M. V. (1999). Academic motivation and the student athlete. *Journal of College Student Development*, 40(2), 151.

Sirgy, M. J., Grzeskowiak, S., & Rahtz, D. (2007). Quality of college life (QCL) of students: Developing and validating a measure of well-being. *Social Indicators Research*, 80(2), 343–360.

Spence, J. T., & Helmreich, R. L. (1983). Achievement related motives and behaviors. In J. T. Spence (Ed.), *Achievement and achievement motives: Psychological and sociological approaches* (pp. 7–74). San Francisco, CA: W. H. Freeman and Company.

TEDx. (2015, Jan. 16). Greg Eells: Cultivating resilience [Video file]. Retrieved from https://www.youtube.com/watch?v=eLzVJVM1BUc

Ting, S. M. R. (2009). Impact of noncognitive factors on first-year academic performance and persistence of NCAA Division I student-athletes. *The Journal of Humanistic Counseling*, 48(2), 215.

Thompson, C., & Gregory, J. B. (2012). Managing millennials: A framework for improving attraction, motivation, and retention. *The Psychologist-Manager Journal*, 15(4), 237–246.

Tracey, T. J., & Sedlacek, W. E. (1982, March). *Non-cognitive variables in predicting academic success by race.* Paper presented at Annual Meeting of the American Educational Research Association, New York, NY. Retrieved from http://files.eric.ed.gov/fulltext/ED219012.pdf

Tuckman, B. W. (1996). The relative effectiveness of incentive motivation and prescribed learning strategy in improving college students' course performance. *The Journal of Experimental Education, 64*(3), 197–210.

Vereen, L. G., Butler, S. K., Williams, F. C., Darg, J. A., & Downing, T. K. (2006). The use of humor when counseling African American college students. *Journal of Counseling and Development, 84*(1), 10.

Watson, J. C., & Kissinger, D. B. (2007). Athletic participation and wellness: Implications for counseling college student-athletes. *Journal of College Counseling, 10*(2), 153–163.

Watt, S. K., & Moore, J. L. (2001). Who are student-athletes? *New Directions for Student Services, 2001*(93), 7–18.

Waxman, H. C., Gray, J. P. & Padron, Y. N. (2002) Resiliency Among Students at Risk of Academic Failure. In *The Yearbook of the National Society for the Study of Education* (pp. 29–48). Chicago, IL: University of Chicago Press.

Wiley, E. W., Shavelson, R. J., & Kurpius, A. A. (2014). On the factorial structure of the SAT and implications for next-generation college readiness assessments. *Educational and Psychological Measurement, 74*(5), 859–874.

Winters, C. A., & Gurney, G. S. (2012). Academic preparation of specially-admitted student-athletes: A question of basic skills. *College and University, 88*(2), 2–9.

Wolverton, B. (2008). Athletes' hours renew debate over college sports. *Chronicle of Higher Education, 54*(20). Retrieved from http://chronicle.com

Woodruff, A. L., & Schallert, D. L. (2008). Studying to play, playing to study: Nine college student-athletes' motivational sense of self. *Contemporary Educational Psychology, 33*(1), 34–57.

Wrisberg, C.A. (1996). Quality of life for male and female athletes. *Quest, 48,* 392–408.

Wrisberg, C. A., Johnson, M. S., & Brooks, G. D. (2000). *Assessing the quality of life of NCAA Division I collegiate athletes: A qualitative investigation* (Unpublished data).

CHAPTER 6

RESPONSE TO INTERVENTION (RtI) AS A FRAMEWORK FOR INNOVATION

Morris R. Council III
University of West Georgia

Mary R. Sawyer
Accelerated Learning Lab of Atlanta, Georgia

ABSTRACT

Response to intervention (RtI) is a popular approach designed for K–12 school settings to systematically ensure learners who present with learning and behavioral needs receive individualized, scientifically validated instruction prior to being referred to special education. The framework is recognized as a tiered, preventative academic model that structures the provision of increasingly intensive interventions to students at-risk for academic failure before they fail. This chapter proposes RtI as an innovative, efficient structure to revolutionize the provision of collegiate academic support for student-athletes. Although most offices of student-athlete support services utilize systems that screen and provide support (e.g., learning specialists, academic counselors) beyond what is available to nonathletic students, far too many student-athletes who present risk factors early in their collegiate

The Collegiate Athlete At Risk:
Strategies for Academic Support and Success, pp. 93–108
Copyright © 2019 by Information Age Publishing
All rights of reproduction in any form reserved.

careers fail to reach graduation or transition away from intensive support on the path to graduation. Offices of student athlete support should use an RtI framework to strategically match the individual's level of need to the intensity of services provided. Doing so will facilitate greater academic success among student-athletes.

We were three years into the new coach's regime, and the detailed plan for athletic dominance which he had so passionately outlined during his interview was coming to fruition. Our team was off to its best start in school history (7–0); the university, fans, and alumni were ecstatic. Those of us working in academic support, however, were experiencing unprecedented stress attempting to match the athletes' accomplishments on the field with their performance in the classroom. Aggressive recruiting and a winning culture led to an increased number of student-athletes who were fully focused on their sport but less prepared academically. We devised a plan to provide intensive supports to our underclassmen (i.e., freshmen), attempting to remediate their academic challenges early-on in their collegiate careers. We were confident this approach would ameliorate the need for intensive resources as the students transitioned into upperclassmen. Our reality was the academic challenges remained for many of the students deemed most at-risk, requiring extended intensive supports that depleted our dedicated staff and valuable resources throughout those students' tenure on campus. (Mid-Major Academic Counselor)

The preceding vignette reflects the pressure felt by many academic support departments to accommodate all student-athletes, and more intensely those at risk for academic failure, with the appropriate resources to meet their needs. It is no secret many student-athletes enter their respective institutions grossly underprepared academically in comparison to their non-athletic peers (Heydorn, 2009), requiring intensive institutional support. In order for support services to be effective, they must be provided consistently and with fidelity. In other words, even robust academic interventions are unproductive when implemented inaccurately or erratically. Unfortunately, providing numerous student-athletes intensive support with integrity requires considerable resources (i.e., qualified personnel and time). According to the National Collegiate Athletics Association (NCAA), no more than two academically at-risk student-athletes should be admitted per academic year (NCAA, 2010). Recruitment is conducted in the best interest of the athletic department and school, often resulting in disregard for the NCAA's recommendation. Enrolling student-athletes on the basis of their athletic ability enables competitive sporting teams that generate revenue and reputations that cannot be overlooked in favor of what is best for individual student-athlete or the academic support office. This chapter proposes the use of response to intervention (RtI) as a framework to assist academic support offices in strategically organizing supports and interventions to better utilize resources and meet the needs of all student-athletes.

WHAT IS RESPONSE TO INTERVENTION (RtI)?

RtI is a model for structuring the delivery and evaluation of school-based interventions, and increasingly it has been implemented across K–12 settings. This academic service delivery process allows educators to scaffold increasingly intensive instructional techniques alongside increasingly sensitive diagnostic measures to ensure all learners have equitable access to and benefit from their education. RtI is based on the public health model of tiered intervention, with an emphasis on tailoring preventative protocols to match an individual's perceived level of risk and presenting symptoms. According to the Center on RtI at the American Institute of Research (National Center on Response to Intervention, 2010), RtI is a framework that:

> [I]ntegrates assessment and intervention within a multi-level prevention system to maximize student achievement and reduce behavior problems. Within this framework, schools use data to: identify students who demonstrate risk for poor learning outcomes, monitor student progress, provide evidence-based interventions, adjust the intensity and nature of those interventions depending on a student's responsiveness, and identify students with learning disabilities or other disabilities. (para. 1)

RtI became a popular framework among educators when the Individuals with Disabilities Education Act (IDEA) was reauthorized in 2004 (Fuchs & Fuchs, 2006; Klingner & Edwards, 2006; Sullivan & Castro-Villarreal, 2013). It was designed to equip student support teams (i.e., school-based professionals who collaboratively address students' academic and behavioral issues) with a problem-solving process to provide two major benefits: (1) improved identification of students requiring special education, and (2) increased early intervention for all children not progressing as expected (Klingner & Edwards, 2006; Proctor, Graves, & Esch, 2012). RtI has facilitated effective intervention by efficiently targeting resources to meet the needs of students in K–12 schools. The framework has received tremendous recognition as a preventative academic model aimed at catching students before they fail (Stewart, Benner, Martella, & Marchand-Martella, 2007). Although its most common use has been to target and improve fundamental skills such as reading (Fuchs & Fuchs, 2006), RtI is a versatile model in academic settings.

An RtI framework is sometimes referred to as a multi-tiered system of support, and it typically consists of three tiers. "Response" in RtI refers to the degree to which individual students master the content delivered via the "intervention" or teaching method. Universal instruction to which approximately 80% of students will "respond" is provided in Tier 1. This tier focuses on the general curriculum and on providing high-quality evidence-based instruction to all learners (Sullivan & Castro-Villarreal, 2013).

Students who do not respond to Tier 1 receive Tier 2 services in addition to Tier 1. The support team meets to identify and analyze the problem (i.e., "nonresponse" in Tier 1), and to plan the next intervention (e.g., small-group instruction, additional practice, another teaching method, etc.) and how it will be evaluated for effectiveness (Fuchs & Fuchs; Sullivan & Castro-Villarreal). Approximately 15% of students will find success in Tier 2; those who do not (about 5% of students overall) are further evaluated and provided with more intensive, individualized support in Tier 3. Students unresponsive to Tier 3 are subject to further evaluation to determine eligibility for special education.

RtI IMPLEMENTATION ESSENTIALS

The versatility of an RtI framework allows for adaption, which allows the needs of interventionists to be met across a wide range of disciplines. In the context of education, there are three primary processes: (a) screening and assessment; (b) intervention; and (c) monitoring of progress. These activities are conducted in light of data-based decisions made strategically by student support or success teams. This section describes characteristics of these key implementation features as they are commonly addressed in academic settings.

Student Success Teams

The student success team is comprised of professionals including the student's current and previous teachers, teachers' assistants, school leaders (e.g., the principal or assistant principal), school psychologists, school counselors, and grade level and special education teacher representatives. These stakeholders collaboratively problem-solve throughout the RtI process to ensure all students are provided with the necessary amount of high-quality, research-based intervention to succeed in the general education curriculum. Together, the student support team engages in ongoing, data-based decision making related to initial student screening and assessment, intervention selection and implementation, and monitoring of student response to intervention. These data-based decisions occur within all levels of RtI implementation (i.e., Tiers 1, 2, and 3).

Figure 6.1.   Data-based decision matrix.

Data-Based Decision Making

At the crux of any RtI framework is data-based decision making. Data analysis occurs recursively at all levels of implementation. Routines and procedures for making decisions are to be established and enforced, with explicit decision rules to determine adequate student progress. The adequacy of the core curriculum can be compared to different amounts and types of instructional interventions through data analysis. The student success team continuously evaluates student data to make intervention decisions and to determine the student's movement up and down in the tiers. For example, when a student achieves academic success at the secondary level of intervention, the degree of supplemental support will be deemed no longer necessary and the student can resume exclusive Tier 1 services. Alternatively, when a student fails to respond adequately at the secondary level of intervention, the student support team must determine more intensive intervention is required and move the student to Tier 3. Careful and timely data analysis allows the student support team to make justifiable decisions related to academic programming and to tweak intervention "dosages" to ensure the efficient, yet effective, utilization of resources.

Screening

The primary purpose of screening students is to identify or predict those who will be at risk for poor academic outcomes, and this element of the RtI process is implemented in Tier 1. Typically, universal screening assessments are brief and conducted with an entire grade level of students. Additional testing can follow for students flagged at the initial screening to corroborate their status of risk. The Center on Response to Intervention at the American Institutes for Research recommends the student support team select evidence-based screening tools that are culturally and linguistically responsive, and care is taken in implementing the measures with reliability (National Center on Response to Intervention, 2010).

Intervention

Interventions differ along the RtI continuum in a variety of ways and can generally be summarized as increasing in intensity as students move into the secondary and tertiary tiers of the framework. Intensity with respect to the ratio of teacher or interventionist to students range from class-wide, whole group instruction at Tier 1 to small groups with a teacher or assistant at Tier 2 to one-on-one intervention implementation at Tier 3. Intervention intensity can also vary in frequency and duration of intervention, level of training of the interventionist, and in the instructional programming and techniques used. Typically, the time, resources, and personnel dedicated to intervention implementation increases as students' progress in the RtI framework.

Progress Monitoring

Student response to primary, secondary, and tertiary interventions is monitored with the purpose of estimating rates of improvement, identifying inadequate progress, and comparing the effectiveness of various approaches. Monitoring progress involves the administration of assessments and other forms of systematic data collection at regular intervals, such as weekly, biweekly, or monthly.

RtI AND COLLEGIATE ATHLETICS

Educators, counselors, and academic support staff owe it to college athletes to provide comprehensive services that enable them to excel in the classroom as well as on the field of play. In the realm of collegiate student-athlete academic support, the RtI framework must be utilized to organize support services. In addition to the potential benefits for student-athletes, this approach relieves stress on departments that are inefficiently or unsuccessfully meeting the needs of their at-risk populations by equipping them with a process to systematically align their interventions and supports with the unique and individual needs of student-athletes. It assists these units by helping them to more efficiently utilize the resources available to them with a better understanding of the needs of student-athletes and ability to make data-based decisions to address those needs.

ALIGNING STUDENT ACADEMIC SUPPORT OFFICES INTO RtI

Student academic support offices are to provide services systematically along an RtI model of multi-tiered support. Each program adapts the model to address the unique needs of the student athlete population, with special attention to the core services they will provide each tier. Special considerations include the support or success team members who are involved at each level, the intervention variations allow for increasing intensity as students move up through the tiers, and the ways in which success teams monitor progress to ensure their system is working. We recommend program leaders create RtI action plans to structure their processes along a 3-tiered continuum.

Tier 1

The focus of Tier 1 is all student-athletes, with the expectation at least 80% of disaggregated groups will not require further intervention. Academic support staff must separate student data by sport, race, and gender to ensure equitable delivery of services across all subgroups at this level.

Student success team. The Tier 1 student support team needs to be comprised of all full-time academic support services office staff. Usually, these individuals include: academic counselors (i.e., individuals who work with student-athletes and university advisors to ensure compliance); advisors (i.e., those who provide support with course scheduling); and university support service staff (e.g., those who provide content tutoring, supervise writing and learning centers, etc.). Most higher education institutions acknowledge before factoring in academic or social readiness, student-athletes will be at-risk for academic failure simply due to the number of responsibilities and time commitments they must juggle. The services provided in Tier 1 must meet 80% of all student-athletes' needs by addressing common issues such as those found with time management, study skills, and accessing novel academic content. Effective Tier 1 implementation allows appropriate allocation of resources and personnel to those student-athletes who present with academic and/or other challenges requiring greater support and remediation.

Screening and intervention. A primary assumption of RtI is data are carefully analyzed and used to make informed, deliberate decisions. During Tier 1, academic support personnel utilize screening data to identify students in need of more intensive support. Student support staff examine the academic profiles of incoming students, identify those who are at-risk for failure in their college coursework, and design monitoring procedures to expedite the timely provision of Tier 2 interventions when those offered at the universal level produce insufficient student response.

Prevention and proactive intervention is the hallmark of RtI, and it is especially important in Tier 1 where the needs of at least 80% of the students overall must be addressed. Institutions of higher education must develop a general group of stakeholders including leadership from the student-athlete academic support office, student affairs, faculty athletic representative, and a liaison from the sports coaching staff. This leadership team needs sole responsibility of conducting a comprehensive screening on every student-athlete to determine their collegiate academic readiness.

Tier 1 screening includes: clearinghouse data (SAT and/or ACT scores, GPA), university academic screeners, academic screeners unique to the academic support office, and demographic narratives (e.g., hometown, strengths, weaknesses, community assets). Screening data collected by the leadership team must provide a comprehensive snapshot of the academic readiness and potential risk for school failure of the learner. Data collected must determine what tier of support will best meet the needs of student-athletes. For example, if a student-athlete is administered an assessment that determines he or she is reading at a fifth-grade level equivalent, support staff will know immediately the student will require more than Tier 1 support.

Progress monitoring. In Tier 1, progress monitoring is comprised of techniques traditionally used to monitor student progress, such as weekly meeting updates, tutor and academic reports, and academic progress reports from faculty. Student athletes who present red flags (i.e., warning signs of at-risk for academic failure) during progress monitoring need to be recommended for Tier 2 services. These red flags consist of student-athletes who chronically:

- struggle to submit assignments on time;
- are late to class and scheduled appointments;

- underprepared for academic activities (i.e., no supplies for class or tutoring); and
- under perform on academic task and assignments.

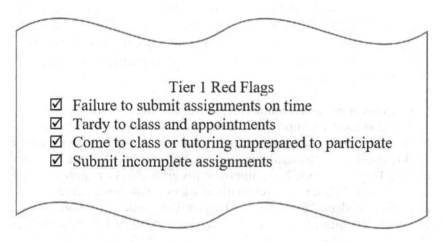

Tier 1 Red Flags
☑ Failure to submit assignments on time
☑ Tardy to class and appointments
☑ Come to class or tutoring unprepared to participate
☑ Submit incomplete assignments

Figure 6.2.   Tier 1 red flags.

Tier 2

The focus of Tier 2 is on students who present a high risk for poor learning outcomes that supersede the services provided in Tier 1. In traditional RtI models, this risk is identified through a screener. Any student-athlete who has been accepted into an institution while failing to meet the entrance criteria of the school must be considered for Tier 2 services in addition to the aid provided in Tier 1.

Student success team. At this level, the student support team needs to be comprised of personnel who are highly skilled in academic coaching. Academic coaching will include one-to-one or small group meetings between the academic coach and the student-athlete. The meetings will assist student-athletes in navigating the university ecosystem, developing and monitoring progress towards academic goals, and supporting them with basic transitional aptitudes (e.g., organizational skills, learning strategies, and health/wellness techniques).

Intervention. The cornerstone of Tier 2 lies in providing support to student-athletes who struggle with the transition from high school to college. These services must meet the needs of an additional 15% of all student-athletes.

Academic coaches need to be able to provide support in:

- Personal care (e.g., sleep and wellness).
- Organization (e.g., notes, course material, monitoring assignments and due dates, creating organizers or planners).
- Time management (e.g., class attendance, tardiness, study time, and budgeting time for assignments).
- Test taking (e.g., Developing preparation materials, self-testing).
- Motivation and attitude (e.g., frustrated, overwhelmed, or perfectionism mentality).

Progress monitoring. Similar to progress monitoring measures in Tier 1, Tier 2 is mostly comprised of traditional techniques used to monitor student progress. These include more intensive progress checks during weekly meetings with academic coaches, in addition to data reported during Tier 1 support. More intensive progress checks require student-athletes to collaborate closely with academic coaches to review their university academic portals (e.g., Banner Web) and institution e-mails. Reviewing this information provides real-time data on how student-athletes are responding to intervention. Academic support offices must also request engagement reports from faculty requesting information on how often students engage in class or with online materials (e.g., frequency and duration of engagement with online academic content).

Student-athletes who fail to respond to Tier 2 intervention will have their supports revaluated by support staff to ensure the accuracy and consistency with which interventions are implemented is adequate and to determine the necessity of increasing the intensity of supports. Only student-athletes who fail to benefit from more intensive Tier 2 supports and have red flags that identify basic academic skill challenges are to be recommended for Tier 3 services. Red flags include student-athletes who:

- struggle to process verbal information;
- have difficulty with higher-order thinking (e.g., inferencing), memory, basic grammar, handwriting, and sequencing; and
- struggles with maintaining focused attention.

Tier 3

The focus of Tier 3 is on individualized and intensive student-athlete support. In traditional RtI models, students requiring this level of support are identified through the screening process conducted in Tier 1, or through a trial-and-error process of finding those who have not responded to primary-

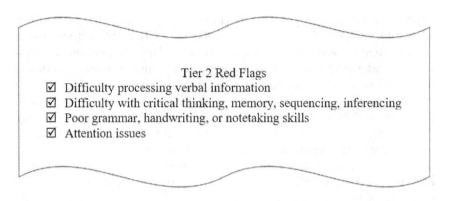

Figure 6.3.   Tier 2 red flags.

and secondary-level prevention. This includes students who have very low levels of achievement, or students with disabilities who have historically required intensive intervention during their secondary education.

Student success team. At this level, the student support team needs to be comprised of intervention/learning specialists who are highly trained to work with student-athletes who present with academic difficulties that supersede the services traditionally provided by post-secondary institutions. Student-athletes with significant academic skill challenges (particularly those with diagnosed disabilities) are arguably an institution's most at-risk population.

> Many student-athletes with disabilities enter their respective institutions un-der significantly lowered admissions standards, oftentimes requiring inter-vention that traditional disability support service offices are not equipped to support. Assuming the student athlete is also not motivated by academic achievement intensifies the level of risk often requiring specialized support for their entire tenure as student-athletes. (Council, Robinson, Bennett, & Moody, 2015, pp. 74–75)

Because of the significant challenges faced by student-athletes in this tier, it is recommended position coaches or personnel from the coaching staff (e.g., academic liaison) be directly involved. Academic support staff are to work collaboratively with the team representative to ensure compre-hensive provision of services across the board.

Intervention. Tier 3 intervention includes intensive and individual-ized instruction in academic skill areas (e.g., reading comprehension and handwriting). This instruction should not be confused with content area tutoring, and rather aim to support student-athletes to a mastery criterion or level suitable for independent academic engagement. Many postsecondary institutions provide support comparable to our Tier 2 recommendations (e.g., content tutoring, time management, etc.). However, without addressing the underlying core skill challenges through more intensive academic remediation, student-athletes receiving such support are unlikely to reap the intended benefits. In fact, the phenomenon of so many profoundly academically underprepared student-athletes entering postsecondary settings is primarily the result of a failure to address fundamental skills in K–12 academic settings. Fundamental skills must be directly targeted in order for student-athletes to be able to access higher level education. Unfortunately, most post-secondary educators do not anticipate or prepare to address the necessity of remediating basic skills. We recommend academic support staff acknowledge this disconnect and be proactive in planning to address these issues at Tier 3.

At Tier 3, student-athletes need to receive intensive intervention adapted to address individual student needs through the systematic use of assessment data, validated interventions, and research-based instruction or behavior support strategies. The coaching staff academic liaison must be involved in the design and implementation of academic support interventions and help implement reinforcement contingencies to keep players motivated and on the track to success. In addition to instruction in skill areas, student-athletes need training in self-advocacy and self-determination.

Progress monitoring. Progress monitoring has to consider student growth in individually identified core skill challenge areas. Curriculum based measurement (CBM) is commonly used within RtI framework applications in K–12 settings. CBM allows the use of simple indicators to determine student development over time (Fuchs, 2016). CBM tasks can be administered briefly and frequently, and there are readily available formats for content areas including reading, writing, and mathematics. We recommend Tier 3 academic support teams identify appropriate CBMs to use to inform their data-based decision making at the individual student level. Additionally, the team must identify other forms of evidence they can use to monitor student progress related to noncore skill intervention targets.

CURRENT BEST PRACTICES

Today, there is minimal guidance in current research literature on how best to provide academic support while preserving confidentiality; although, the NCAA outlines some basic recommendations serve as a foundation for the universal tier. These recommendations target critical issues academic support staff leverage to positively impact student-athlete academic performance. Staff will use Table 1 to monitor their adherence to the guidelines.

The NCAA recommendations provide universal support to all student-athletes and are identified as Tier 1 supports. This is what the tiers would look like with additional RtI recommendations.

Table 6.1.
NCAA Recommendations Within an RtI Model

Recommendation	Completed	Not Competed	In Progress
Tier 1			
Supervised study hall available for a minimum of 8 hours per week.			
Minimum of 4 hours of need-based subject-specific tutoring			
Academic progress reports from faculty three times per semester (75% desired return rate)			
80% student-athlete enrollment in incoming student transition program			
Weekly meeting with coaching staff to review student-athlete performance (staff requirement)			
Access to weekly meeting with academic counselor or advisor			
Mandatory study sessions included in travel itinerary			
Establish 4-year graduation plan (staff)			
Tier 2 (Recommended)			
Weekly meetings with academic coach or mentor			
Tier 3 (Recommended)			
Weekly meetings with learning specialist			
Weekly meetings with position coach/liaison			

These recommendations must be integrated into the culture of the institution with explicit academic routines understood and valued to ensure all student-athletes are aware of and understand expectations. Many academic support offices currently offer similar services but do not frame them as a universal foundation for all student-athletes within a larger, more comprehensive model of support. Further, most programs lack an evaluation criterion to measure their efficacy to, at the basic level, meet the needs of 80% of all student-athletes. It is critical for support programs to acknowledge a large portion of their student-athletes will not be academically successful without additional intervention.

IMPLICATIONS FOR STAFF

The strategic alignment of services and personnel within an RtI framework is likely to reduce burnout among staff. Academic support staff play a significant role in the lives of student-athletes (particularly those at risk for school failure) and usually work in highly demanding settings. Typically, these personnel are highly educated with most earning masters degrees prior to their entrance into the profession (Council et al., 2015). Unfortunately, many academic support personnel are tasked to complete duties outside the boundaries of their professional training which can lead to frustration and burnout. For example, staff with degrees outside of the education profession (e.g., sport management) should never be tasked to support student-athletes who require Tier 3 services unless they can demonstrate the capacity to effectively provide intervention. However, staff who are highly trained to support student-athletes in Tier 3 should not have the sole responsibility of providing Tier 2 supports to student-athletes.

> I taught special education at the high school level for over a decade and have successfully worked with students ranging from gifted to those who were functionally illiterate when we first started working together. When I applied for this position (Athletic Learning Specialist), I felt it would be an amazing opportunity to influence young adults who had been failed by K–12 education but had a life changing opportunity through collegiate athletics. During my interview that is how the position was presented to me, "an opportunity to use my vocation to change lives". Unfortunately, soon after I began the position I found myself being tasked to help students monitor assignments and report on their grades. In my mind, this was bonafide babysitting considering my skill set. I mean really, why would you hire someone with my experience to make sure adults were submitting assignments. Sad part was, I could have really helped them if given the opportunity to do what I was trained to do. (Power Five Conference Learning Specialist)

In the above narrative, a learning specialist was asked to perform the task of an academic coach. The description represents the frustration felt by academic support staff when their skillsets are underutilized or are not aligned within a model that target services to the individualized needs of student-athletes. Simply aligning staff to tiers has the potential to increase the effectiveness of services provided to student-athletes and decrease burnout. Decreasing employee burnout over time will strengthen the overall services provided by the academic support department and significantly reduce expenditure for new hire search committees. Finally, associating staff within an RtI framework can assist leadership in (1) aligning staff with the services needed from student-athletes and (2) assign fiscal value to employees based on services rendered to student-athletes.

CONCLUSION

The RtI framework offers student academic support offices with an innovative service delivery model for providing expedited, efficacious interventions. The model is flexible and can be adapted for a variety of contexts; the key is to establish a systemic implementation protocol understood and easily executed by staff at all levels. Adequate planning can ensure the framework is implemented in a way that ensures responsible use of resources. Typically, the RtI process begins at Tier 1, but students in higher education who have established academic profiles can be placed at the appropriate tier to address their needs from the start.

It is important to note tiers represent services not students; students must never be referred to by the tier of services they are currently receiving. RtI is not a fixed placement and students can move across tiers. The goal is for all students to have meaningful access to the universal, Tier 1 services available. As needs arise and are identified, students need supplemental services at Tier 2 or 3. Those services need to be provided with the intention of moving them back to Tier 1. Similarly, students who are identified for Tier 2 or 3 upon entering their postsecondary institutions should not remain at this point throughout their enrollment. Rather, effective services at the secondary or tertiary level enable students to become successful at the primary level.

The RtI framework enables non-academic leadership to comprehensively provide academic services and communicate effectively to stakeholders. As mentioned above, a student-athlete should never be labeled based on the tier of services she or he is provided. Instead, the student-athlete will have a detailed explanation as to why he or she is receiving specific assistance and the ultimate goal of the department is to graduate all student-athletes at Tier 1. Student-athletes can better conceptualize how their time in academic support offices is being utilized when the RtI structure of service provision is clearly communicated. This framework also provides a systematic but simple methodology for explaining the help rendered by your office to coaches and those who work with the student-athletes on the field. Transparency and a systematic structure ensures (1) student-athletes receive services based on individualized need, and (2) staff are qualified to provide services based on student need. The RtI model also ensures student-athletes who are most at-risk receive opportunities to develop fundamental academic skills that will lead to independence.

REFERENCES

Council, M., III, Robinson, L., Bennett, R., III, & Moody, P. (2015). Black male academic support staff: Navigating the issues with Black student-athletes. In R. A., Bennett III, S. R., Hodge, D. L., Graham, & J. L. Moore III (Eds.), *Black males and intercollegiate athletics: An exploration of problems and solutions* (pp. 69–89). *Diversity in Higher Education, Vol. 16*. Bingley, England: Emerald Group Publishing Limited.

Fuchs, L. S. (2016). Curriculum-based measurement as the emerging alternative: Three decades later. *Learning Disabilities Research & Practice, 32*, 5–7.

Fuchs, D., & Fuchs, L. S. (2006). Introduction to response to intervention: What, why, and how valid is it? *Reading Research Quarterly, 41*(1), 93–99.

Heydorn, M. (2009). Explaining the graduation gap-athletes vs. non-athletes: A study of the Big Ten and Missouri Valley Conferences. *The Park Place Economist, 17*(1), 11.

Klingner, J. K., & Edwards, P. A. (2006). Cultural considerations with response to intervention models. *Reading Research Quarterly, 41*(1), 108–117.

National Center on Response to Intervention. (March 2010). *Essential components of RTI—A closer look at response to intervention*. Washington, DC: U.S. Department of Education, Office of Special Education Programs, National Center on Response to Intervention.

NCAA division l academic progress rate improvement plans best practices addressing the most common eligibility and retention issues. (2010, September 23). Retrieved January 5, 2017, from http://www.meacsports.com/pdf9/2493486.pdf

Mellard, D. F., & Johnson, E. (2008). *RTI: A practitioner's guide to implementing response to intervention*. Thousand Oaks, CA: Corwin Press

Proctor, S. L., Graves Jr, S. L., & Esch, R. C. (2012). Assessing African American students for specific learning disabilities: The promises and perils of response to intervention. *The Journal of Negro Education, 81*(3), 268–282.

Stewart, R. M., Benner, G. J., Martella, R. C., & Marchand-Martella, N. E. (2007). Three-tier models of reading and behavior A research review. *Journal of positive behavior interventions, 9*(4), 239–253.

Sullivan, J. R., & Castro-Villarreal, F. (2013). Special education policy, response to intervention, and the socialization of youth. *Theory Into Practice, 52*(3), 180–189.

CHAPTER 7

STAYING ENGAGED

Faculty Mentoring Student-Athletes

Darren D. Kelly
The University of Texas at Austin

Robert A. Bennett III
Denison University

ABSTRACT

This chapter explores the potential for male faculty and staff members to serve as mentors to at-risk student-athletes within higher education. Student-athletes are the most visible students of the entire student population at these institutions and often influence how students are viewed and treated by other faculty, students, and the university communities at large. Based on empirical research, classroom and administrative experience, this chapter will discuss the impact of faculty mentoring on student-athletes enrolled in college and provide solutions for administrators and faculty members to utilize in their efforts to help guide these students towards achieving athletic, academic, and personal success.

The Collegiate Athlete At Risk:
Strategies for Academic Support and Success, pp. 109–120
Copyright © 2019 by Information Age Publishing

Given the high demands on their time, talent, and energy toward their mandatory and voluntary sport responsibilities, student-athletes have limited opportunities to engage in significant extracurricular and professional development opportunities. According to the National Collegiate Athletic Association (NCAA), student-athletes typically spend 34 hours per week on their athletic activities and commitments (NCAA, 2016). For high profile athletes in sports like Division I football, the athletic time commitment increases to about 42 hours per week. Given student-athletes must also attend classes, study hall and other academic sessions with athletic academic support staff, it leaves little time to engage in activities with faculty and staff outside of class to enhance their educational experiences. It is critical athletic departments find ways to free up the time demands of student-athletes and provide further opportunities to interact with faculty and staff on college campuses through mentoring programs and initiatives.

Student-athletes also experience feelings of isolation from the rest of the student body and academic community given their athletic schedule and obligation (Benson, 2000; Kelly & Dixon, 2014). They lack the time necessary to get fully integrated into academic and campus life and often must forgo opportunities to get greatly involved in cocurricular and extracurricular activities. Student-athletes' interaction with faculty typically takes place during classes and the occasional visit to office hours unless there are prescribed opportunities to interact with faculty outside of the classroom that work with a student-athletes' schedule, which typically consists of classes, tutoring, practice, conditioning, and athletic competition. This limited faculty interaction provides a missed opportunity for student-athletes to feel as though they are a part of the academic community and can lead to further stigma and isolation from their peers.

This chapter will focus on the benefits and merits of faculty and staff mentoring at-risk student-athletes and provide suggestions and models for practitioners to emulate and implement. First, we will discuss the origins of mentoring, mentoring programs, and how mentoring has had an impact on various industries, including higher education. Second, we will analyze existing models of university faculty/staff-student-athlete mentoring programs in the United States. Third, we will provide recommendations and steps on how to create faculty/staff—student-athlete mentoring initiatives, programs and/or events.

Faculty-Student Interaction Enhances the Undergraduate Experience

Given their duties as teachers in the classroom and leaders of research teams, faculty have a great opportunity to greatly improve the academic experience of undergraduate college students in a variety of ways. When faculty have significant and meaningful interaction with students, it can lead to various positive outcomes such as increased academic motivation (i.e. effort towards achieving academic success), cognitive growth, social integration, and retention (Jaasma & Koper, 1999; Rugutt & Chemosit, 2009; Trolian, Jach, Hanson, & Pascarella, 2016). Although these are some strong and positive outcomes, students cannot gain these benefits from attending classes alone. The quality and frequency of faculty interaction with students are factors in the strength and impact of the relationship between the two parties (Comeaux & Harrison, 2007). Thus, faculty must be genuine and intentional in their efforts to connect with students, especially student-athletes.

Outside of coaches and other athletic support staff, faculty have the opportunity to spend a significant amount of time with student-athletes during classes and office hours and encourage their academic development. Similar to their non-athlete student counterpart, student-athletes also can benefit from spending time with faculty members inside and outside of the classroom (Umbach, Palmer, Kuh, & Hannah, 2006). Faculty who have encouraged student-athletes, particularly male student-athletes, to explore and attend graduate school positively influenced their academic success (Comeaux, 2011). Comeaux and Harrison (2007) advocated for more academic and social activities where student-athletes can interact with faculty members outside of the classroom and develop stronger relationships between the two groups and further integration into the academic setting. Yet while there is great promise for the faculty-student-athlete relationship, there are concerns that must be addressed and dealt with before any relationship is developed.

Researchers have discovered faculty student-athlete interaction differs among student-athlete populations particularly by race/ethnicity. When it comes to race/ethnicity, the major differences are typically found between Black and White male student-athletes. Comeaux and Harrison (2006) found faculty who provided assistance with academic skills and developing professional goals had a more positive association with White student-athlete's academic success than Black student-athletes' success. Additionally, the type of interaction with faculty is also significant when it comes to the experiences of Black versus White student-athletes (Comeaux & Harrison, 2007). A major factor that contributes to these differences are the stereotypes and stigma associated with Black student-athletes and their influence on faculty attitudes. It has been well-established within the scholarship on this topic that student-athletes, Black student-athletes in particular, face an inordinate amount of negative stereotypes and racism on large, historically White university campuses (Kelly, 2012; Simons, Bosworth, Fujita, & Jensen, 2007; Singer, 2005) which often are manifested in negative perceptions among faculty members (Engstrom, Sedlacek, & McEwen, 1995; Sailes, 1993). Thus, when it comes to the prospect of mentoring student-athletes, faculty need to be in-tune with student-athletes' needs—especially those with educational vulnerabilities. As such, mentors should consider the backgrounds of the students they assist.

What Is Mentoring?

While mentoring has become a useful and popular tool for support-ing students in higher education, it is critical to have an understanding of what mentoring is for it to be effective. The concept of mentoring was originally developed in the 1970s and 80s in the field of business, human resources, organizational behavior and education (Germain, 2011). While there is not a consensus definition of mentoring among all researchers, mentoring is typically known as a relationship between a senior person and a younger protégé who often can serve as a role model, assist with personal or career development, and provide social support (Kram, 1985). The tra-ditional model of mentoring is a one-on-one dyadic relationship between two people where a senior person (mentor) helps a junior organizational member (mentee) reach organizational and/or personal goals. The end result is the achievement of other desirable outcomes that improves the developmental relationships of individuals (Higgins & Kram, 2001).

Mentoring has been utilized to achieve various positive outcomes for both mentor and mentee participants, especially in both the business and academic setting. Since student-athletes are often compared to employees in an organization it is only fitting to utilize this concept to enhance their experiences as students and athletes. Academically, students in mentoring relationships have been found to have higher GPA than their counter-parts who did not have a mentor (Sorrentino, 2006). Additionally, other outcomes for students include increased satisfaction with their university (Baker, Hocevar, & Johnson, 2003; Koch & Johnson, 2000), personal iden-tity development (Erkut & Mokros, 1984), and an expanded social network (Johnson & Huwe, 2003). Student-athletes at-risk can greatly benefit from these outcomes as it will help fight against feeling isolated from the rest of the university and empower student-athletes to greater explore their academic identity outside of sport.

While the one-on-one mentoring dyad is the most well-known mentor-ing model, other models for mentoring have emerged over the years. Many are familiar with informal mentoring—the original relationship formed through an organically meeting between two individuals, while formal programs, which include multiple mentors have grown in popularity. Composite mentoring is a strategic selection of varied mentors by a protégé where each mentor serves a different need and provides specific direction for that protégé (Packard, 2003). This form of guidance was derived from an earlier model called constellation mentoring, which involved multiple advisors serving different purposes for the mentee (de Janasz & Sullivan, 2004). Each mentor serves a unique need with the mentee while there is not coordination among them. Essentially, sport has the potential to serve as a site for mentoring not only between coaches and athletic department staff and student-athletes, but also faculty and student-athletes too.

Current Mentoring Models for Student-Athletes

Multiple student-athlete mentoring models exist within higher education. They serve the purpose of assisting with personal, academic, intellectual and career development. These models are specific to the university setting and the specific student-athlete population but may be helpful when considering a mentoring model for student-athletes at a major college or university. Practitioners should examine these models and evaluate whether a similar or modified model will be best suited for their institution.

Athletic Department Led Mentoring—CSU John Mosely Student-Athlete Mentoring Program

Colorado State University (CSU), a land grant state university located in Fort Collins, CO, created the John W. Mosely Student-Athlete Mentoring Program in 2011. Named after the first African American football player at CSU, the mentoring program was a collaboration between the CSU athletic department and the Black/African American Cultural Center "designed to assist student-athletes by serving as a resource while strengthening time management skills, encouraging academic success, enhancing leadership opportunities, and creating a sense of belonging and connection to the campus and its surrounding community" ("Lt. Col. John W. Mosely Student-Athlete Mentoring Program," 2018). The program connects student-athletes with faculty and staff on campus and also brings in former athletes and other alumni for various personal and professional development events. The Mosely program provides regular interaction with faculty, staff and alumni who are able to relate to the experience of being a student-athlete with rigorous time demands and are able to help the participants better acclimate themselves to the challenges of attending a large, public institution.

The Mosely program is funded through the Colorado State University athletic department under the leadership of Senior Associate Athletic Director of Diversity, Inclusion and Engagement, Albert Bimper. A former CSU student-athlete, Bimper is also an associate professor of ethnic studies at the university and is able to bridge the athletic and academic worlds together based on his own experience and scholarship. Bimper raised the profile of the Mosely Program and expanded it to serve more student-athletes and incorporate more mentors. As an athletic department initiative, the program has an advantage of being accessible to student-athletes and getting buy-in from other stakeholders of the athletic department including coaches and academic support staff

Collective Uplift: A Faculty Driven Program at the University of Connecticut

Founded in 2015, the Collective Uplift program at the University of Connecticut was established by Joseph Cooper to developmental opportunities for student-athletes of all backgrounds beyond the traditional academic and athletic setting ("Collective Uplift," 2018). Other goals from the program include fostering holistic development through programs and activities, integrating individuals into campus culture, and providing opportunities for student-athletes to have impact on their society through service and outreach. Faculty participate in many different aspects of the Collective Uplift program such as the professional development activities, real talk panel discussions, and the Making a Difference by Diversifying Educators (MAD^{2}E) program. Student-athletes have real interactions with faculty members through these events creating informal mentoring opportunities and developed relationships over time.

Collective Uplift is a faculty-led program which allows for professors to readily buy into the program given its direction under a fellow researcher and faculty member. Additionally, being led by an African American male, it can likely attract student-athletes of color, and African American student-athletes in particular, to participate in the program. However, Collective Uplift, like other faculty driven programs, has continued to bridge the gap between the academics and the athletic department to earn respect and buy-in from athletic department stakeholders. Often this is a challenge for faculty members looking to work with student-athletes as athletic departments are very sensitive to the time constraints of student-athletes and may be hesitant to working with outside entities. Cooper has done a tremendous job making his program research-based and academically sound while being a good partner with the athletic department and making the program accessible to student-athletes.

AAMRI: A Diversity Initiative Mentoring African American Male Students and Student-Athletes

Established in 2012, the African American Male Research Initiative (AAMRI) is a faculty-driven, academic initiative based on evidence-based practices to help promote academic excellence among African American males at The University of Texas at Austin. Housed in the Division of Diversity and Community Engagement, the program serves both African American male students and student-athletes by providing additional support through personal, academic, and professional development activities and events and connecting them to other supplemental programs and opportunities on and off campus. For example, AAMRI hosts a weekly program called Power Hour. This gathering serves as a time for Black male students and student-athletes to have discussion about current events and pertinent topics directly impacting. Power Hour events feature discussions led by graduate students and faculty assisting African American undergraduate students and student-athletes in navigating the complexity of a large, public historically White university. These weekly events provide multiple points of interaction between faculty/staff and student participants and allow for the organic creation of faculty mentor relationships.

Another AAMRI program, the annual Black Student-Athlete Summit, creates larger opportunity for student-athletes to interact with faculty members. The summit is a 3-day gathering of student-athletes, faculty, staff and other community members to discuss the issues facing Black student-athletes on college campus across the nation. This forum also allows for practitioners and scholars to share best practices on addressing matters pertinent to Black student-athletes with the intent of developing quality educational experiences for this student population. The same came be done for student-athletes at-risk. The summit not only draws student-athletes and faculty from the host campus, but also brings in participants from universities from around the world providing an expansive networking opportunity for student-athletes and faculty. The summit has not only resulted in the sharing of research and best practices, but it has also created undergraduate research collaborations between student-athletes and faculty and opportunities for student-athletes to attend graduate school under the guidance of faculty and staff who attended the conference.

PEAK Mentoring: Understanding the Athletic and Academic Experience at OSU

Formed in 2016, the Paths to Educational Attainment and Knowledge, or PEAK Program is a structured mentorship-based initiative designed to strengthen the collegiate experience and post-graduation trajectories for student-athletes at The Ohio State University (OSU). This population, especially members of the OSU football and basketball teams are often the focus of race-centered discourse concerning student-athletes at-risk of academic failure (Blackman, 2008; Hodge, 2015). The program was designed to strengthen the matriculation and postgraduation trajectories for such student-athletes. PEAK addresses challenges student-athletes face throughout the duration of their collegiate experience (i.e., first semester in their freshmen year to postgraduation). The program is open to all student-athletes. However, Black male student-athletes the targeted group as research has shown that they are less likely to graduate than their collegian peers (Gaston Gayles, Crandall, & Jones, 2015; NCAA, 2016).

In particular PEAK is organized between the Todd A. Bell National Resource Center on the African American Male, OSU's Department of Athletics, Student Athlete Support Services Office (also known as SASSO), and OSU's faculty, graduate students, administrators, and staff. This collaborative effort maximizes the collegiate experience for student-athletes providing resources for high quality educational and life lesson experiences. For example, roundtable discussions are organized to give students, staff, and faculty the opportunity to engage in discourse around pertinent topics. There are also social events like video game tournaments that have shown to help build camaraderie among participants and mentors. The PEAK Program's tenets are grounded in research that indicates student-athlete engagement in educational activities and meaningful relationships with faculty and campus personnel are key factors in academic success (e.g., Charleston, Jackson, Adserias, & Lang, 2015; Martin, Harrison, Stone, & Lawrence, 2010). Further research indicates mentoring is important to academic success and personal/career development of Black male student-athletes (Charleston et al., 2009; Kelly, Harrison, & Moore, 2015).

Recommendations for Fostering Faculty-Student-Athlete Mentoring Relationships

This chapter focuses on the benefits of faculty mentoring undergraduate student-athletes and highlights existing models at American, public universities. While these programs may not be easily duplicated or copied, there are some best practices and qualities from each model and the research to help implement opportunities for faculty to mentor student-athletes. First, it is imperative for all persons invested in student development and success to understand the populations with which they work. Creating faculty-student-athlete mentoring programs or mentoring opportunities in a vacuum does not automatically result in positive outcomes for student-athletes. Athletic personnel, faculty and other staff involved in the creation of initiatives must do their due diligence to better comprehend their student-athlete population and learn about their specific needs. Thus, those whom are establishing mentoring program for their particular student-athlete populations must have a good relationship with them and seek direct input from the student-athletes themselves to prevent a scenario where they are working in isolation.

Second, care must be given to the selection of the most suitable and capable faculty members for any mentoring program. These faculty members should be vetted, and suggestions should be gathered from student-athletes. If a faculty member teaches undergraduate classes and have not taught student-athletes before, then they may not likely be a good fit to be a mentor given their lack of interaction with student-athletes (intentional or unintentional) and unfamiliarity with the student-athlete experience. Faculty members should not be included in a mentoring program if they are overly invested in the athletic aspect of student-athletes' lives and seek to enhance their own status by affiliating with the athletic department and high-profile student-athletes. Additionally, there should be a healthy mix of faculty from diverse racial, gender, and socioeconomic backgrounds to allow for the maximization of their ability to relate to a diverse group of student-athlete participants.

Third, establish clear boundaries for mentoring relationships for both the faculty mentors and student-athletes. It is critical those persons who work with student-athletes at-risk understand the purpose of the mentoring relationships so trust can be established and provide opportunities for either the mentor or mentee to exit the relationship. Additionally, student-athletes, who may not be very trustworthy of new relationships, need to feel comfortable about sharing their personal thoughts and issues with their mentor and identify what they share will be kept in confidence.

Fourth, mentoring programs cannot rely on a traditional one-on-one matching of faculty mentors with student-athletes. While the one-on-one mentoring relationship is powerful, it also has the potential to put too much onus on one faculty member to assist a student-athlete with their holistic development. Additionally, if the one-on-one relationship finds to be unbeneficial and the two parties cannot relate, it may result in the student-athlete not wanting to continue with the program at all. Creating opportunities for student-athletes to have multiple mentors may take pressure off of one faculty mentor to serve as a resource in all facets of life and allow several mentors to have an impact on a student-athlete in a variety of ways and provide unique guidance in different areas. This setup also mitigates the risk of a negative experience with one mentor by allowing the student-athlete to be able work more closely with another faculty member with whom they can relate.

Last, host and organize regular group faculty mentoring events to create opportunities for faculty-student interaction and relationship development. By doing this, it takes pressure off mentors to create the opportunities and gives student-athletes the chance to not only meet with one of their assigned faculty and staff members, but also get to know others who are attending the events. Additionally, it allows for consistent interaction during the semester or quarter and aids student-athletes in making this a routine part of their schedule.

ACKNOWLEDGMENTS

Darren D. Kelly, Division of Diversity & Community Engagement. This research was supported in part by the African American Male Research Initiative a program of the Division of Diversity and Community Engagement. Correspondence concerning this article should be addressed to Dr. Darren D. Kelly, African American Male Research Initiative (AAMRI), 2304 Whitis Ave., G4600 Austin, TX 78712.

REFERENCES

Baker, B. T., Hocevar, S. P., & Johnson, W. B. (2003). The prevalence and nature of service academy mentoring: A study of navy midshipmen. *Military Psychology, 15*, 273–283.

Benson, K. F. (2000). Constructing academic inadequacy. *Journal of Higher Education, 71*(2), 223–246.

Blackman, P. C. (2008). The NCAA's academic performance program: Academic reform or academic racism? *UCLA Entertainment Law Review, 15*(2), 225–289.

Charleston, L. J., Jackson, J. F. L., Adserias, R. P., & Lang, N. M. (2015). Beyond the game™: Transforming life outcomes of Black male collegiate student-athletes. In R. A. Bennett III, S. R. Hodge, Graham, D. L., & J. L. Moore III, (Eds.), *Black males and intercollegiate athletics: An exploration of problems and solutions* (pp. 285–306). Bingley, England: Emerald Group Publishing Limited.

Collective Uplift. (2018, March 11). Retrieved from https://wp.uplift.education.uconn.edu/our-goals/

Comeaux, E. (2011). Examination of faculty attitudes toward Division I college student-athletes. *College Student Affairs Journal, 30*(1), 75–87.

Comeaux, E., & Harrison, C. K. (2006). Gender, sport and higher education: The impact of student-faculty interactions on academic achivement. *Academic Athletic Journal, 19*, 38–55.

Comeaux, E., & Harrison, C. K. (2007). Faculty and male student athletes: racial differences in the environmental predictors f academic achievement. *Race Ethnicity and Education, 10*(2), 199–214. doi:10.1080/13613320701330726 de Janasz, S. C., & Sullivan, S. E. (2004). Multiple mentoring in academe: Developing the professorial network. *Journal of Vocational Behavior, 64*, 263–283.

Engstrom, C. M., Sedlacek, W. E., & McEwen, M. K. (1995). Faculty attitudes toward male revenue student-athletes. *Journal of College Student Development, 36*(3), 217–227.

Erkut, S., & Mokros, J. R. (1984). Professors as role models and mentors for college students. *American Educational Research Journal, 21*, 399–417.

Gaston Gayles, J., Crandall, R. E., & Jones, Jr., C. R. (2015). Advising Black male student- athletes: Implications for academic support programs. In R. A. Bennett III, S. R. Hodge, Graham, D. L., & J. L. Moore III, *Black males and intercollegiate athletics: An exploration of problems and solutions* (pp. 45–68). Bingley, England: Emerald Group Publishing Limited.

Germain, M. L. (2011). Formal mentoring relationships and attachment theory: Implications for human resource development. *Human Resource Development Review, 10*(2), 123–150.

Higgins, M. C., & Kram, K. E. (2001). Reconceptualizing mentoring at work: A developmental network perspective. *Academy of Management Review, 26*, 264–288.

Hodge, S. R. (2015). Black male student-athletes on predominantly White college and university campuses. In R. A., Bennett III, S. R., Hodge, D. L., Graham, & J. L. Moore III (Eds.). *Black males and intercollegiate athletics: An exploration of problems and solutions* (pp. 121–149). Bingley, England: Emerald Group Publishing Limited.

Jaasma, M. A., & Koper, R. J. (1999). The relationship of student-faculty out-of-class communication to intructor immediacy and trust and to student motivation. *Communication Education, 48*, 41–47.

Johnson, W. B., & Huwe, J. M. (2003). *Getting mentored in graduate school*. Washington, DC: American Psychological Association.

Kelly, D. D. (2012). *Constructing the framework for mentoring African American male student-athletes at predominately White institutions of higher education* (Doctoral of Philosophy Dissertation). The University of Texas at Austin, Austin, TX.

Kelly, D. D., & Dixon, M. A. (2014). Successfully navigating life transitions among African American male student-athletes: A review and examination of constellation mentoring as a promising strategy. *Journal of Sport Management, 28*(5), 498–514. doi:10.1123/jsm.2012-0320

Kelly, D. D., Harrison, Jr., L., & Moore, L. N. (2015). Answering the call: Black male faculty mentoring Black male student-athletes. In R. A., Bennett III, S. R., Hodge, D. L., Graham, & J. L. Moore III (Eds.). *Black males and intercollegiate athletics: An exploration of problems and solutions* (pp. 239–260). Bingley, England: Emerald Group Publishing Limited.

Koch, C., & Johnson, W. B. (2000). Documenting the benefits of undergraduate mentoring. *Council on Undergraduate Research Quarterly, 19*, 172–175.

Kram, K. E. (1985). *Mentoring at work : Developmental relationships in organizational life*. Glenview, IL: Scott, Foresman.

Lt. Col. John W. Mosely Student-Athlete Mentoring Program. (2018, March 11). Retrieved from http://www.baacc.colostate.edu/john-w-mosley-student-athelete-mentoring-program

Martin, B. E., Harrison, C. K., Stone, J., & Lawrence, S. M. (2010). Athletic voices and academic victories: African American male student-athlete experiences in the PAC-Ten. *Journal of Sport & Social Issues, 34*(2), 131–153. doi:10.1016/j.econedurev.2005.10.008

National Collegiate Athletic Association. (2016). *NCAA GOALS study of the student-athlete experience: Initial summary of findings.* Retrieved from http://www.ncaa.org/sites/default/files/GOALS_2015_summary_jan2016_final_20160627.pdf

Packard, B. W. (2003). Student training promotes mentoring awareness and action. *Career Development Quarterly, 51*(4), 335–345.

Rugutt, J., & Chemosit, C. C. (2009). What motivates students to learn? Contribution of student-to-student relations, student-faculty interaction and critical thinking skills. *Education Research Quarterly, 32*(3), 16–28.

Sailes, G. A. (1993). An investigation of campus stereotypes: The myth of Black athletic superiority and dumb jock stereotypes. *Sociology of Sport Journal, 10*, 88–97.

Simons, H. D., Bosworth, C., Fujita, S., & Jensen, M. (2007). The athlete stigma in higher education. *College Student Journal, 41*(2), 251–273.

Singer, J. N. (2005). Understanding racism through the eyes of African American male student athletes. *Race, Ethnicity and Education, 8*, 365–386.

Sorrentino, D. M. (2006). The SEEK mentoring program: An appication of the goal-setting theory. *Journal of College Student Retention, 8*(2), 241–250.

Trolian, T. L., Jach, E. A., Hanson, J. M., & Pascarella, E. T. (2016). Influencing Academic Motivation: The Effects of Student-Faculty Interaction. *Journal of College Student Development, 57*(7), 810–826.

Umbach, P. D., Palmer, M. M., Kuh, G. D., & Hannah, S. J. (2006). Intercollegiate athletes and effective educational practices: Winning combination or losing effort? *Research in Higher Education, 47*, 709–733.

EPILOGUE

On October 13, 2017 the Committee on Infractions under the National Collegiate Athletic Association (NCAA) announced they were unable to conclude that the University of North Carolina (UNC) violated any NCAA academic rules. Prior to this ruling UNC had been accused of providing student-athletes with extra academic benefits through "paper classes" that required minimal effort. It was determined that these paper courses existed in the university setting for 18 years from 1993 until 2011. Although UNC has been cleared of all wrong doing, the fact remains in this scenario and many others across the country, student-athletes who present academic risk of school failure receive a collegiate experience defined by academic loopholes, lowered expectations, and the prioritization of progress toward degree over the quality of education earned.

Collegiate athletics has provided many opportunities for students with academic and social risk factors to enter into institutions of higher education and pursue professional opportunities within and outside of sport. This is largely due to the complex ecosystem of athletic departments comprising various units that range from compliance, administration, athletic training, strength and conditioning, coaches, academic support, etc. This book focuses specifically on the environment in which academic support takes place. Although there are multiple units within collegiate athletes that support student-athletes, there is only one that focuses on the student in student-athlete. For this reason, the environment has significant value

The Collegiate Athlete At Risk:
Strategies for Academic Support and Success, pp. 121–122
Copyright © 2019 by Information Age Publishing

to the mission of amateur athletics and this is particularly true for student athletes at risk for academic failure.

Often when discussing student athletes at risk for academic failure there is an overemphasis placed on the students without adequate exploration of the environment established to support them. For those who work in the academic environment it can be easily characterized by negative features (e.g., high stress, poor work life balance, thanklessness) with few recommendations to improve the conditions of personnel or the student-athletes they support. The purpose of this book is to move the conversation away from monitoring and information delivery to begin a conversation on establishing best practice in the world of collegiate athletic academic support. Through best practices we can begin to meet the true vison of the student-athlete without leaving those at-risk behind.

ABOUT THE AUTHORS

THE EDITORS

Morris R. Council III, PhD, assistant professor of literacy and special education in the College of Education, University of West Georgia. He received his BS in education and MEd in curriculum and teacher leadership; both from Miami University. He earned his PhD in special education and applied behavior analysis from The Ohio State University. Dr. Council has several years' experience working as a tutor, learning specialist, and football academic specialist for various DI student-athlete support service offices providing hands on experience supporting the needs of collegiate student-athletes who demonstrate academic and social risk. He has also written and presented extensively in the area of student-athlete academic support, most recently "Black Male Academic Support Staff: Navigating the Issues with Black Student-Athletes" (Council, Robinson, Bennett, & Moody, 2015).

Samuel R. Hodge is a professor in the Department of Human Sciences in the College of Education and Human Ecology, The Ohio State University. He is the recipient of the America Scholar Award sponsored by the Research Council of the Society of Health and Physical Educators (SHAPE) of America as well as recipient of the Adapted Physical Activity Council's Professional Recognition Award (American Alliance for Health, Physical Education, Recreation & Dance; AAHPERD); E. B. Henderson Award and Charles D. Henry Award (AAHPERD); and Distinguished Scholar Award

(National Association of Kinesiology in Higher Education). His scholarship focuses on diversity, disability, and social justice in education and sport. He has published extensively including such articles as: "Theorizing on the Stereotyping of Black Male Student-Athletes: Issues and Implications" (Hodge, Burden, Robinson, & Bennett, 2008); and "Brown in Black and White—Then and Now: A Question of Educating or Sporting African American Males in America" (Hodge, Harrison, Burden, & Dixson, 2008). Professor Hodge is also coeditor of the book titled, *Black Males and Intercollegiate Athletics: An Exploration of Problems and Solutions* (Bennett, Hodge, Graham, & Moore, 2015); as well as coauthored chapters in edited books including such titles as: *Historically Black Colleges and Universities' Athletes and Sport Programs: Historical Overview, Evaluations, and Affiliations* (Hodge, Bennett, & Collins, 2013); *The Journey of the Black Athlete on the HBCU Playing Field* (Hodge, Collins, & Bennett, 2013); *African American Males and Physical Education* (Hodge & James-Hassan, 2014); and *Health, Nutrition and Physical Activity* (Hodge & Vigo-Valentín, 2014).

Robert A. Bennett III, is an assistant professor in Health, Exercise and Sport Studies at Denison University. A native of Decatur, Georgia, Bennett graduated from Morehouse College with a bachelor of arts degree in history with honors where he was also a member of the football team. He earned his master of arts degree and doctor of philosophy from The Ohio State University in History. His research interests are: sport history; the intersection of race, gender and sport; student-athlete identity; and athletes and activism. He is coeditor of *Black Males and Intercollegiate Athletics: An Exploration of Problems and Solutions*, and has publications in *Racism in College Athletics*, the *Journal of Sport History, The Journal of African American History, Boyhood Studies* and the *Journal for the Study of Sports and Athletes in Education*. Bennett is married to his wife Gisell and they have a son Amari Lumumba Ade.

THE AUTHORS

Susie C. Bruhin is the director of operations at Internet Marketing Expert Group, Inc. in Sevierville, Tennessee. A native of Mooresville, North Carolina, Bruhin graduated Magna Cum Laude from Marshall University with a bachelor of arts degree in elementary education where she was also a member of the women's swimming and diving team. She graduated summa cum laude with her master of arts degree from Marshall University in Reading Education and later earned a Professional Project Management Certificate from the University of Phoenix. She dedicated her early career to working with at-risk students of all ages who faced unique learning challenges including learning disabilities and ADHD. During her time at Marshall, Bruhin served as the assistant director of the Marshall University Higher Education for Learning Problems (H.E.L.P.) Program, and later served as a learning specialist at the Thornton Athletics Student Life Center at the University of Tennessee–Knoxville. Although no longer working in the education field, Bruhin continues to volunteer her time teaching basic literacy skills to local at-risk students.

Stephon Fuqua is a senior athletics academic counselor in the Student-Athlete Support Services Office (SASSO) at The Ohio State University. In his role, he oversees the academic progress of football student-athletes and facilitates personal and professional development programming geared toward building their leadership and decision-making skills. Throughout his career in higher education, Mr. Fuqua has always found ways to demonstrate and build his leadership skills within various settings. Prior to joining the Buckeyes, he worked as an associate director in the Student-Athlete Support Services Office at the University of Cincinnati and various advising and mentoring positions at Eastern Kentucky University. Mr. Fuqua earned a bachelor's degree in business and organizational communication from the University of Akron in 2008 and in 2010, he received a master's in Sport Administration from Eastern Kentucky University. He is currently working towards completing his PhD in Health Education at the University of Cincinnati.

Ralph Gardner, III, PhD, is an emeritus professor of special education/applied behavior analysis at The Ohio State University in the Department of Educational Studies. Dr. Gardner's research focuses on instructional interventions for improving academic outcomes for urban children who are at risk for school failure and children with mild/moderate disabilities. Dr. Gardner's research has appeared in some of the field's leading peer-reviewed journals. Dr. Gardner has received several awards for teaching excellence from The Ohio State University, including the Alumni Distinguished Teaching Award (highest teaching award at the university). He has been invited to present at U.S. and international universities on academic instructional practices, special education, and multicultural issues.

Joy Gaston Gayles is professor of higher education at North Carolina State University. Her research focuses on college student access and success, most notably for student-athletes and women and underrepresented people of color in STEM fields. Gaston Gayles work is published widely in top journals in the field. Further, Gaston Gayles has received numerous awards for her contributions to higher education.

Darren Kelly is the deputy to the vice president for diversity and community engagement and an assistant professor of instruction of kinesiology at The University of Texas at Austin. In his role, Dr. Kelly oversees programs under the academic creativity and design and university culture portfolios such as TRIO programs, the Multicultural Engagement Center, and precollege academic readiness programming among others. He is the cochairperson of the annual Black Student-Athlete Summit—a national conference addressing critical issues facing Black student-athletes across the world. Additionally, he serves as the codirector of the Urban Economic Development in South Africa Study Abroad Program—the largest and most diverse study abroad program in the country—which recently took a record 81 students to Cape Town in 2018. Dr. Kelly received his undergraduate degree in finance and marketing from the University of Virginia in 2004, his MA and PhD in Kinesiology with specialization in Sport Management from The University of Texas at Austin in 2009 and 2012. His research interests center on African American male student and student-athlete academic and professional development. He is married to his wife Paige and enjoys watching sports with his two sons, Devin and Davis.

Robert Lang is a doctoral student in educational leadership, policy, and human development, with a concentration in higher education, in the College of Education at North Carolina State University. His research interests revolve around issues of equity and diversity in STEM programs at the post-secondary level as well as program evaluation using quantitative methods of analysis. In addition to Lang's studies and research at NC State, he serves as a research intern at the Center for Responsible Lending.

Emily Newell, PhD, is an assistant professor of sport management at the University of Southern Maine's School of Business. Her research centers on the intersection of sport and higher education, with a particular focus on minority populations. Newell's primary research is related to the international student-athlete experience at American universities, and has been presented and published at the NCAA Inclusion Forum, the North American Society for Sport Management, and NACADA: The Global Community for Academic Advising, among others.

Prior to entering academia, Newell worked in various positions in intercollegiate athletics at both the NCAA and The Ohio State University, including as an Athletic Academic Counselor at Ohio State.

Ezinne Ofoegbu is a doctoral student in Educational leadership, policy, and human development, with a concentration in higher education, in the College of Education at North Carolina State University. Ofoegbu earned a master's degree from the University of Southern California. Her research interests focus on issues and problems in intercollegiate athletics.

Lori S. Robinson serves as the director of Learning Center Services in the Nye Center for Student-Athlete Services at Texas A&M University (TAMU). Prior to coming to TAMU, Robinson served as a learning specialist and academic counselor at the Thornton Athletics Student Life Center at the University of Tennessee–Knoxville. Prior to Tennessee, Robinson also served as a learning specialist and assistant tutor coordinator at the Cox Communications Academic Center for Student-Athletes at Louisiana State University (LSU). Robinson, a former student-athlete and Ronald E. McNair scholar, holds a BS in sport management, as well as a MS in Instructional design development and evaluation both from Syracuse University. Lori S. Robinson is currently a doctoral candidate in Educational Leadership Research and Counseling with an emphasis in higher education administration, educational research methodology, and reading instruction at LSU. Robinson's research interests include the transition of student-athletes from the secondary education system to a 4-year institution, and the holistic development of student-athletes primarily at Division-I colleges and universities.

Mary Sawyer, BCBA-D, is Founder and CEO of TEAM Coaching, an organization dedicated to advancing applications of behavior analysis in education through training and dissemination of best practices. Dr. Sawyer is also co-owner of Fit Learning Atlanta, where she serves as director. Additionally, Dr. Sawyer is adjunct faculty for the applied behavior analysis (ABA) master's program at Georgia State University. She is passionate about utilizing the science of learning and behavior to rapidly accelerate academic outcomes and to create nurturing environments in which individuals of all ages thrive. Dr. Sawyer blends expertise in coaching educators and parents to problem-solve and engage in evidence-based practice, multi-tiered systems of support such as response to intervention and positive behavior support (PBS), and instructional design. She holds a PhD from The Ohio State University, and an MA in special education, an M.A. in ABA, a graduate certificate in PBS, and a BS in elementary education from the University of South Florida. Furthermore, she is certified in teaching elementary education, exceptional student education, and english speakers of other languages.

CPSIA information can be obtained
at www.ICGtesting.com
Printed in the USA
LVHW081048180722
723695LV00004B/120